Library of Congress
2025923604
Copyright 2025
ISBN 979-8-218-71338-6
First Edition
Created in the United States of America

Dedicated to Our Ancestors

From the Land of Trolls
Nisser & Krumkaker

Holiday and Traditional Recipes,
Folktales, Ancestry,
and Folk Art

By

Norwegian-American Cousins
Christy Roe and Linda Danielsen

TABLE of CONTENTS

Chapter #1. Ancestry   page 1

Chapter #2. Norwegian Holiday Desserts   page 39

Chapter #3. Traditional Norwegian Recipes   page 69

Chapter #4. Folktales   page 97

Chapter #5. Folkways   page 123

Index   page 164

Introduction

Only books don't make one wise

Bare bøker gjør ingen kloke

Climbing up the stairs, as adults, in the big yellow house seemed a bit mysterious, knowing that the last time we did this, our great grandmother was still alive. She had been in bed with a broken hip, just in the nearest bedroom. My brother Steve had made a plaster-of-Paris handprint for her in kindergarten. I being a scared, chatty, four year old was told to be as quiet as I could. We made a brief child's connection with a great woman who had come to Seattle 60 years earlier all the way from Norway.

Now, as adults attending a reunion nearby, we were anticipating the search through an old trunk that we were told contained some things we might be interested in. Always wanting a deeper connection to our cousins, our parents' parents and so on, this seemed like a good place to learn more. Our curiosity seemed to explode as we searched through the letters, photos, and old yearbooks. Steve came across a letter to my grandmother, Harda, from a Daniel Danielsen with a Norway address. He immediately wrote to Daniel and waited. However, the letter wasn't known about until Daniel's daughter, Marit, found it after her father had passed away, sorting through his things. Marit gave her cousin Linda Danielsen, Steve's information and the correspondence began revealing that we share the same great grandfather, Hans Kristian Sorensen.

In the 1950s and 1970s, Daniel Danielsen visited his relatives; aunts, uncles, and cousins, in Seattle, Washington when his cruise ship docked. The Erdevig family enjoyed visiting with him.

Linda Danielsen and Christy Roe connected from families and friends. They enjoy some of the same traditional Norwegian recipes, holiday treats, and both went to "Pioneer Girls" when they were very young. Each of the mothers made Krumkaker and gave it away as gifts. They each have 4 brothers, too. Where as Linda's family and relatives settled in New York and Florida, Christy's relatives settled mostly in the Pacific Northwest with a stop in Chicago along the way. Her family, known to travel a lot, has put down roots in Washington, Connecticut and California. They both share 1st and 2nd cousins in Lillesand, Norway.

This book started out as a collection of recipes that we remember from growing up Norwegian-Americans. We still use the recipes in some of our cooking, However, the more we shared in photos, stories, and history the more we wanted to write the information down.

As you read this perhaps you will be remembering, too.

Christy Roe

Norwegian American Cousins Remember

Ancestry

Borte bra, hjemme beste

Away is good, Home is best

Chapter 1

NORWAY COORDINATES

60.4720 LATITUDINAL

8.4689 LONGITUDE

NORWAY'S CAPITAL: OSLO

HOME of the NOBEL PEACE PRIZE

The Nobel Peace Prize is decided by and given annually by a committee of five from Oslo, Norway. This award recognizes individuals and organizations that significantly contribute to conflict resolution and peace promotion. Four United States Presidents have been honored with this; Barack Obama, Jimmy Carter, Woodrow Wilson, and Theodore Roosevelt. In 1964 Martin Luther King Jr. was awarded the Nobel Peace Prize for his leadership of the Civil Rights Movement. This held the goal toward achieving racial justice through non-violent actions. United States is the holder of the most Nobel Peace Prizes. Norway has received 14 at the time of this publication.

HOW LINDA DANIELSEN
AND
CHRISTY ROE ARE RELATED

HANS KRISTIAN SORENSEN   married   KAREN DANIELSDATTER
GREAT GREAT GRANDPARENTS

Ole Hansen (Erdevig) + Josine Olsen (brothers) Daniel Hansen + Bergitte Pedersdatter
GREAT GRANDPARENTS

Harda Erdevig + Walter Foard (cousins) Hans Danielsen + Mathilde Thomasdatter
GRANDPARENTS

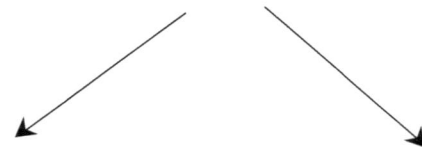

Carol Foard + Phil Roe (2nd cousins) Alice Johnsen + Thomas Danielsen
PARENTS

Christy Roe (3rd cousins) Linda Danielsen

Some of the mystery studying the surnames of my relatives in Norway, is because it wasn't until 1923 any definite rules for regulating occured. In Norway, Linda and I share a great great grandfather whose last name was Sorensen. My great grandfather took the last name of Hansen, (Son of Hans) and Linda's great grandfather did, too. When my great grandfather Ole came to United States he changed his last name to Erdevig. Linda's great grandfather used the last name Danielsen. My grandmother, Harda Erdevig, was a cousin of Hans Danielsen, Linda's grandfather. And so on.

Here are the Laws on Norway's Personal Names:

• Only last names legally acquired by ancestry, marriage, or other means could be used.
(I think occupational=smith (y), taylor, etc.)

• Last names based on the father's given name with with a suffix identifying gender (sonn, son, sen for males; datter or dotter for females)

• The name of the farm or place of residence if the person, his parents, or grandparents were the owners.

Between 1840 and 1920, nearly one-third of the total population of the Nordic region migrated to the United States. The earliest arrivals in Linda's family settled near the East Coast, while Christy's family left for the Midwest and far West, the Puget Sound region. They worked on farms, in mines and mills, in fisheries and logging camps. Over time, many entered professional life and some became national leaders. Today more than 10 million Americans are descended from immigrants from five Nordic countries.

Supposedly, 10% of the 4.3 million Americans that claim Norwegian heritage reside in Washington State. Many who came to work in the fishing industry arrived to the small community of Ballard. That was true of my great grandfather, Ole, before building his house in Woodway, an area now called Edmonds.

When Norwegians immigrated from their homeland at the turn of the century to the United States, it would make sense that those in agriculture would head to the mid-west where there is a lot of farmland. The sailors, fishermen, and boat builders would naturally want to head to oceans, lakes, and rivers. (East Coast and Pacific Northwest Coast)

Ole Erdevig was quite brave and adventurous to travel to Seattle, Washington from Norway. According to census information he was a ship builder in Norway, but in the United States he did many things to provide for his family; store merchant, rancher, builder of boats and houses. Although electricity wasn't that common yet until the 1930s, Ole prepared his house that he was building in Woodway (Edmonds) for his family, in the 20s, for electricity. He, with Josine, fathered 6 children and raised them in one of the most beautiful places i n Seattle, overlooking Puget Sound. They had a player organ/piano in their living room which fascinated me.

Norwegians used their farm names to clarify their identity when conducting official business or traveling, as mentioned previously. Here is an example of that: Hans Kristian Sorensen, our great great grandfather, bought the Snelldalen Farm from his wife's brother. Ole and Karen owned Snelldalen (house land, and farm) originally called Gisslebakke. Included in the purchase was a piece of marshland called Hestemyre. Hans developed the land as much as possible, farming it.

Unfortunately during WWII, many properties were taken over and controlled by German soldiers. Hans B. Danielsen, Harda's cousin, was stuck in the Far East navigating his cargo ship and was unable to return home to Norway.

On a tragic somber note, Adolf Danielsen, son of Hans, was walking on a dirt road with his younger brother, Thomas, when the Gestapo seized him and put him in Jail. Adolf Danielsen, had been picked as one of the young leaders in the Norwegian Resistance. Adolf Danielsen was probably 20 years old at the time. Of course the Norwegian Resistance was against the occupation of Norway or any country by the Germans during this time.

Thomas, Linda's Father, has retold this story, including the news that his brother had been moved from Oslo to a concentration camp in France. He died 4 years later.

CR

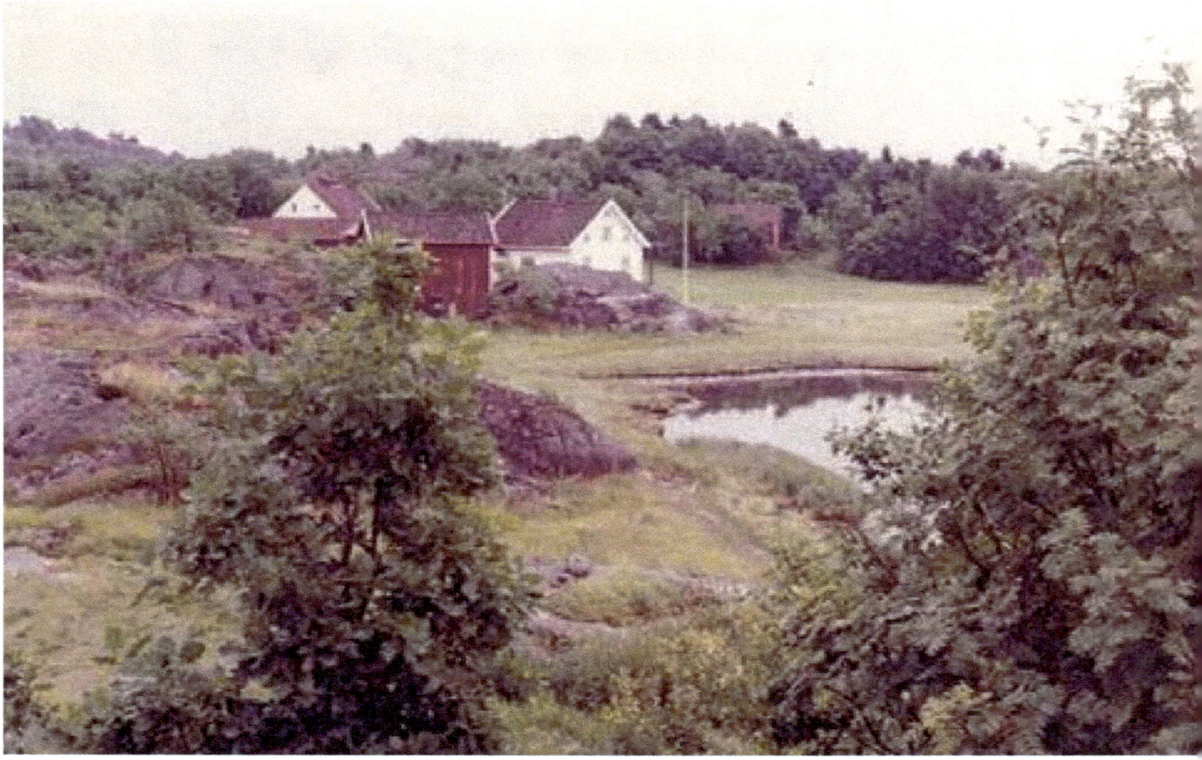

photo by Linda Danielsen

Stuthei – This is the homestead that Karl Stuthei built and where my grandmother, Gudrun was born. It is on the Island of Justøya, right outside of Lillesand

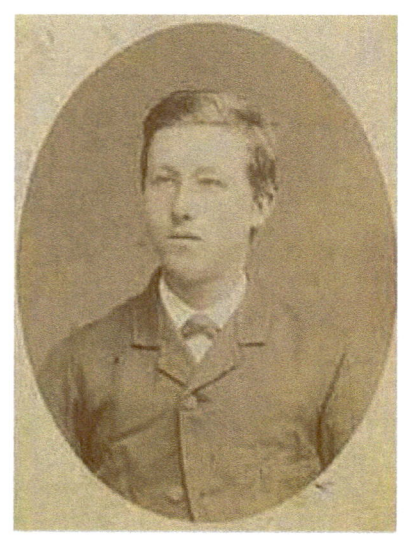

Karl Tønnesen ("Stuthei")

My great-grandfather, Karl Stuthei, became good friends with Gabriel Scott and Nils Kjaer, two of Norway's most famous authors during the early 1900s. Both authors visited Brekkestø, (today a popular cycling route) with their families in the summer. Brekkestø, was the town where my grandmother (on mother's side), Gudrun, was born. She was born on the homestead, Stuthei, which her father had built for his family. Karl Stuthei was a fisherman. Each evening after fishing he would stop by Gabriel and Nil's homes to give them fresh caught fish and lobster. He never accepted money from them. They became good friends, sharing meals and boat rides. Gabriel Scott even vacationed one summer at Stuthei with his wife and two boys. However, soon after that Karl had a tragic accident, one in which he eventually died from the injuries.

Nils Kjaer upon hearing about Karl's accident sent a letter with money for the fish he had been given over the years from Karl. (of course the money was to help with the accident.) Writing back to his friends, Karl said, "Jeg skal dø, kjære veneer, men lev, lev dere!" Roughly translated "I will die, my dearest friends, but you live, and you live well!"

Nils' wife writes that whenever she gets depressed and dissatisfied with how things are going in the world, she takes out Karl's letter and reads it.

I have heard from many people, who knew my great-grandfather, what a wonderful man he was. He was caring, kind, charismatic, and generous even though poor himself. I can't help but feel that Gabriel Scott based some of the book "Marcus, The Fisherman", on my great-grandfather, Karl. After all, he wrote this famous book while vacationing in Brekkestø.

LD

The Good Life In Snelldalen

I am very curious about the lives of my great great grandfather, Hans Kristian Sorensen and his wife Karen Danielsdatter. They lived in Snelldalen, Norway, which is considered Lillisand, now, as part of the Høvåg Parish. Hans was skilled with wood working and carpentry. The census also says that he was a farmer. Snelldalen was a part of a larger farm, called the Erdevig farm. (This is where Hans Kristian's sons took their last name from when they immigrated to America.) Hans' son Daniel became a sea captain on the Atlantic Ocean and Norwegian Sea. Another son, Ole Hansen eventually left for Seattle via Illinois and built his house overlooking Puget Sound up on a hill in Edmonds, Washington. Marit, a cousin in Lillisand today, recommended that reading the book, "Marcus The Fisherman", might give one a glimpse into our great great grandparents' life and environment. Also, the author of this book, Gabriel Scott was friends with Linda Danielsen's great grandfather, Karl Tonnessen. We think Hans might have known Gabriel's father.

The character Marcus talks about his garden of rhubarb, onion, carrots, turnips and gooseberry. He grew sage for his tea, lilac bushes for the visual beauty and sweet aroma, and had the sound of the Wheatear Bird, for his early mornings.

Did Hans and Karen enjoy these same things on the Erdevig

Farm? Their lives so simplistic, but probably were most difficult and disciplined. Mackerel, cod, ling, and lobster in season could be caught and sold in a outdoor market in Lillisand. Perhaps my relatives purchased these items or caught them themselves in a beautiful inlet or fjord.

Dolphins, whales and abundance of sea life all surrounding Norway's coast must have been so enjoyable for everyone.

CR

Lillesand Harbor 2016, photo by Linda Danielsen

Hans Danielsen's Family

Hans Danielsen Family 1938

Mathilde and Hans Danielsen were born, raised, and married in Norway. Even though Daniel Hansen, father to Hans Danielsen, emigrated to Chicago, he left his wife, Bergitte and children back in Norway until he could save up the money to bring them over. He died before that happened. Therefore, Hans Danielsen was raised in Norway, at Nepetrø. They had 6 children, one being Linda's father, Thomas Danielsen.

A cousin, Mathilde Heldal, was one of the cooks to the Kennedy family for over 25 years. She traveled with the family between Hyannis Port and West Palm Beach. However, she spent the summers with her family in Norway. Even then, she was often called back to cook for a special occasion.

There is a story of Mathilde Heldal forgetting her passport at the airport to fly into the States. When the White House was called, the current President, J. F. Kennedy, told the airport security that it was ok for Mathilde to board and travel. After that, she never had a problem at the airport again.

Linda recalls visiting her relative, Mathilde, working in Florida. Linda was in her early teens, but was quite in awe with the family as she roamed the family compound.

Here's my grandmother, Harda Erdevig, on
her honeymoon cruise with new husband,
Walter Foard, on their way to Japan.

Harda Caroline Erdevig was born January 1st, 1899 in Seattle, Washington. She had 4 sisters; Jenny, Jo, Rebecca, and Edna with one brother, Otto. Her parents, Josine and Ole, from Lillesand, Norway, met and married in Illinois. Then they relocated to the town of Ballard. In the census it said that Ole was a rancher. He did build the family house up on a hill in Woodway over looking Puget Sound. Norwegians were reminded of their home in Norway with views of the Olympics, Mt. Rainier, and the Sound. The family had a piano and loved singing to music they liked (and even wrote). Three of the sisters; Rebecca, Harda, and Edna, worked downtown at the Union Bank of Seattle at 2nd Avenue and Pine (now the Boeing Bank). Jenny and Otto left for San Francisco in 1925.

My Grandmother Harda, a stenographer, met Walter, the Vice President of Union Bank, and developed a serious relationship. They married, honeymooned in Japan and settled on the family property in Edmonds overlooking the Puget Sound. They had three children; Walter, Olyn and Carol, my mother. I loved to visit my Grandmother Harda and enjoyed her visits to our family. We would spend time in the kitchen baking Fattingmann and other Norwegian cookies and desserts. My grandmother was a kind and generous person. She loved to garden and also volunteered her time. She and my mother spoke to each other in Norwegian when my mother was growing up and often through the years.

CR

Erdevig House

Edmonds, Washington

Erdevig family at "The Big Yellow House" in Edmonds, WA.
Back row center is Harda and middle row center is Carol.
Photo taken in the early 1940's

Daniel Hansen's ship he sailed called, The Magdalene.

Hans Sorensen was a farmer, fisherman, and builder as he lived near the sea. Is it any wonder that his sons, grandsons and great grandsons would have a love for the sea, too? Daniel Hansen, son of Hans, was both a sailor, ship's captain, and ship's carpenter. He sailed around the world, also! Hans Danielsen, son of Daniel, was superintendent of Lillesand Seaman's School between 1914-1925. Thomas and Ole sailed ships and left Norway for Florida, Washington, and even New Zealand. Daniel Danielsen, Linda's Uncle, was the first to sail a cruise ships into the Lillesand fjord in the 1980's. He also sailed around the world, cruising the Atlantic and Pacific Oceans.

LD

Cruiseshippen "Royal Viking Sky"
Daniel Danielsen's ship (Linda's Uncle) In Lillesand Harbor.

Daniel Danielsen, grandson of Daniel Hansen (from Snelldalen) and uncle to Linda was a ship's captain. When he was in the Port of Seattle, Puget Sound, my grandmother, Harda, would often go visit him for lunch on his cruise ship docked in Seattle, Washington.

CR

Captain Daniel Danielsen with his sister-in-law, Alice Danielsen.

My mom, Alice, would meet "Onkel" Daniel when he came into Port Everglades in Ft. Lauderdale. My dad would meet him, too (before my dad died). They would take my uncle to our home in Ft. Lauderdale for a home-cooked meal. It was always such fun to see him!!

LD

This is the Danielsen Family Reunion photo. It was taken by Daniel Danielsen's son, Arne Daniel Danielsen, in front of the house at Nepetrø in Lillesand. It was the summer of 2015. These are Linda's 1st cousins and their

families. That is, basically the offspring of Mathilde and Hans Didrik Danielsen and Linda's grandparents. Hans Danielsen was the son of Daniel Hansen, who is from Snelldalen, and the brother of Christy's great grand father Ole Hansen Erdevig.

Hi, Christy

Hope this finds you well and full of the joy and peace of our Savior.

So . . . here is the book I spoke about ... the one that Marit Danielsen told me about. The author, Gabriel Scott was born of Norwegian parents in Scotland in 1874 but then the family moved to Hovag, Norway in 1881 when Gabriel's father became the parish priest (state church of Norway). Our great grandfather, Ole, grew up not far from the church and would have worshiped there until he left for America in 1886. I'm quite sure he would have known Gabriel and his parents.

So ... the story in this book of an old fisherman (fiction but I guess that he is based on a man or men the author knew) takes place here in the Hovag (pronounced "Hoovaug") area not far from Lillesand. I will be interested to talk with you about the book when you finish reading it. This is your copy ... I have my own. Perhaps Christina would be interested also.

Love to you,
Steve

Photo and letter by Steve Roe, Lillesand, Norway

Lillesand

This church is in Lillesand. A number of Carol Foard Roe's relatives are buried in it's graveyard.

This church is about 500 years old, so Ole Hansen Erdevig (Christy's great grandfather) would have worshiped here before he left for America. This church is in Høvåg, about 9 miles by water from downtown Lillesand and is now, for government purposes, considered part of Lillesand.

This is an old mill where Carol Foard Roe's great grandmother, Karen Danielsdatter Sørensen, would have brought grain or oats grown by her family, to have it ground into flour. She would have walked here from the family home, Snelldalen, about a mile and 1/2 away.

Steve and Lynne were given a personal tour with Marit of the Lillisand Museum built about 1860.

Arthur and Birgit Thorkildsen, Lillisand, Norway, July 1995
Birgit is Carol Foard Roe's second cousin &
Arthur and Birgit are Linda Danielsen's aunt and uncle.

"Nepetrø is where my Tante Birgit lived until she died. It is also the
birthplace of my father and all his siblings."

LD

25

In 1891 Susan 8. Anthony and Abigail Scott Duniway led a crusade through the territories of Washington and Oregon that eventually led to form the Washington Women Suffrage Association. Washington received statehood in 1889. Even at this time it had a liberal view of equality and women's rights compared to other states. Washington State permanently granted women the right to vote in 1910, as did four other states. It has been said that Black women were granted the Right-to-Vote as well, although most would wait decades for the priveledge to do so. The 19th Amendment gave women the right to vote August 18, 1920 across the nation.

Perhaps these changes in society, including WWI and WWII, brought up very strong women like my grandmother and her sisters, too. Jo, the oldest of the Erdevig sisters, attended Teacher's College in Bellingham. She went on to teach in the Yukon, meeting and marrying a Canadian man, Charles Stone. There were stories of the one room school house in Dawson's Creek amid the Gold Rush Territory. Jo often welcomed the children with muddy feet into the schoolhouse because there were no sidewalks. There were also surprises in the cannery food, no rules yet or regulations. Aunt Jo enjoyed watching the Northern Lights and seeing moose, caribou, grizzly bear and wild Dall sheep. These sheep are known for their large curled horns. Upon her return she taught in Edmonds and Port Orchard. My mother, Carol, was very young to accompany Jo on the ferry to teach. However, she remembers that she helped her aunt stoke the fire In the fireplace, early, before school started. Maybe that's why my mom got a head start on her education before entering first grade in Edmonds. The three Erdevig sisters; Rebecca, Edna, and Harda worked at the Union Bank on 2nd Avenue and Pine Street, downtown Seattle. It is now Bank of Boeing. Right near there was "The Bon", the department store that most everyone loved to go to. It became quickly the first modern store with an Art Deco architect style and was put in the National Register of Historic Places. I have fond memories of going to eat lunch while shopping with Aunt Jo, my grandmother Harda, and my mom, Carol. Later it became Macy's on 3rd Avenue and Pine. Another wonderful store was Frederick & Nelsen's. (Nelson was a Norwegian) They sold these wonderful chocolate truffles that my family thoroughly enjoyed; Frango Mints. They were bought for any special occasion.

CR

Jan Carol Simonsen wrote a new book titled, "Brooklyn Girl, Growing Up Norwegian in New York City". I felt like it was my biography. I read it all in one day. Everything was so similar to me as to the main character in this book. It made me remember so much from my youth. Especially down to the small fact that she talked about going to Kleinfeld's on 3rd Avenue or Lapskaus Boulevard, to help her cousin get her wedding dress. Hedda "Kleinfeld", the owner who I knew really well, talked to the main character saying, "don't worry about getting the dress altered because we have the best seamstress in NYC." This was my grandmother who worked for the Kleinfelds for 25 years as the Head Seamstress. The difference in the book's character and myself was that my family moved to Huntington Station when I was 6 years old and her aunt, uncle and kids moved to Huntington Station, Long Island. I went to the same church I was baptized in as she did and sometimes to the 66th Street Church. We went most every Sunday to Bethel Lutheran Church in Huntington Station. The camps they ran in the summers were amazing, including Pioneer Girls. Every page in the book made me remember something about my youth.

LD

- Brigit and Adolf had no children each, and are no longer living.

- Hans Marius Danielsen 1924-1988 (children: Inger Grete, Hans Gunnar, Ellen and Erik)

- Rolf Danielsen 1933-1988 (children: Thomas, Henrik, and Inger Elisabeth)

- Daniel Danielsen 1922-1998 (children: Kristin, Marit, and Grethe)

- Thomas Emil Danielsen 1926-1974 (children: Linda, Lloyd, John, Glenn, and Thomas)

Hi, Christy

Above is copied from Marit's family tree.

We met Marit and Grethe who are children of Daniel Danielsen.

We met Kristen's husband Jan Erik Tanberg and son Kjetil. (She is no longer living). And ... Son Arne Daniel and wife Inger Sophie with 2 kids. Mathielde and Elise.

We also met Thomas, son of Rolf, who took us for a boat ride.

We took a bus to Flekkefjord, where your great grandma, Josine Erdevig was born. It was pretty quiet when we visited, as it was a Sunday, and I wasn't able to find relatives.

I still make a lot of Norwegian food-especially at Christmas; Krumkaker, Lefse, Julekake, Rullepolse, Norwegian Pancakes, Norwegian Meatballs, Fattigmann, etc.

Josie Lehde
2nd Cousin to Christy Roe
Written after a cruise to Norway

From left to right: Grete, Linda F., Marit, Inger Grete, and Josie

Flekkefjord Waterway Marina

Visiting Edmonds seemed a frequent event for our family. In between our dad's assignments with the U.S. Navy. Our family would show up Winter or Summer. Later, 2 of my younger brothers, with their families, would put down roots as adults in the Northwest. Steve and I have more memories visiting in our younger days.

Once on Aunt Jo's property, when we were quite young, we would collect an egg or two from the chicken coop. We'd slide down the hay loft with the barn kittens, and avoid running into the 2 cows, Daisy and Bossy. Sometimes, we would venture further, holding onto the large cable that when from the top of the hill down to the beach. There were the train tracks to cross, too, at the bottom of the hill. Did our mother have any idea what we were doing at the time? Not sure. I wonder if my mother and her two brothers, Wally and Olyn had the same kind of freedom growing up.

Uncle Wally had an old Ford Model T pick-up truck that we got to ride in. He would point out various woodland creatures; fox, raccoon, and even a bear once. (Or so he said) Unfortunately, I wasn't always looking in the right direction so I missed most sightings. Uncle Wally said he taught my mother, his younger sister, how to drive that truck with a stick shift. I was impressed. On one occasion Wally had asked Carol to drop him off and drive the truck home. She had not gotten her license yet. Brave mom.

Wally took Steve fishing, too. Nearby where there was a flowing stream and lots of rocks. Steve was more interested in climbing big rocks or throwing the little pebbles.

Our second cousins, children of Edna and Harold Lehde, also made quite an impression on us. Steve got driving instructions from his second cousin Davey. He said Steve needed to keep his foot on the pedal to keep the car from rolling down the hill. He believed him. Davey, Andy and Johnny had what we would call today a "Garage Band". Johnny on the drums, the other two on guitar and keyboard. Turns out it was a loud one. I did visit the group and thought they were great. Johnny even tried to teach me how to play the drums.

One summer, camping in a cousin's back yard with Linda, Josie, and Dea in Lynnwood, the hoots of an owl could be heard, slimy slugs felt beneath bare feet, and the exaggerated rumor of bear sightings kept me awake most of the night. Had a bear ever been in the neighborhood? Most probably years before. And later on a hike I did see a small brown bear off in the distance.

I share Linda's excitement of experiencing a big city, her with New York City and for myself, Seattle. I loved window shopping with my Grandmother Harda or my Aunt Jo. There was a health food store, like a soda fountain with counter top and stools, for fresh carrot drinks and other healthy items. It was a must stop for us. This could've been Seattle ahead of it's time with alternative health options or part of the Scandinavian influence on health or both. I have thought the later.

Later, experiencing the Space Needle, for the World's Fair in the early 60s, the Art Museums, Music Venues and theatre on 5th Avenue was such a big deal for myself and family. We had just come back from Argentia, Newfoundland where the Naval Base was about a mile square.

But all the trips around Seattle when I was young, my favorite was to take the Bainbridge Island Ferry to Poulsbo, known as "Little Norway". It is a quaint village town on the water with a view of Mt. Rainer. The restaurants and bakeries always have a Scandinavian selection. Eating lunch and enjoying the Norwegian bakery items was such a treat.

On November 29th, 1981 this poem appeared in one of the local Seattle newspapers. It was basically a Christmas ad for one of the main department stores for downtown Seattle. This is what Marty DeGrazia wrote of his mother's poem.

"My mother worked in the advertising department for The Bon Marche for the majority of her life. She left briefly in the 80's to work for the completion, Nordstrom, and then Frederick's & Nelson. This enabled her to double her income. Hefheart was always at The Bon. Forty years ago she penned this poem for Frederick & Nelson's."

The windows on Pine are a youngster's dylight,
and the Frango Cookie Factory is a delectable sight.
Bears measuring, stirring, baking all day.
They love it so much, you can't tear them away.
The store is just brimming with fashions and toys,
things for the home, for good girls and boys.
We'll help with your shopping, even wrap and send.
Just give us a list of what you can spend.
The beauty of Steuben, and Waterford too,
china from Aynsley are all a delight,
to slip under the tree this Christmas night.
Porcelain from Boehm, so lifelike and true,
beloved by all ... St. Nicholas too.
Do meet our doorman, so jolly and bright.
He'll help with your packages from morning til night.
Dash down the escalator, and see what you'll find,
a bakery, pasta, and candy, homemade.

You'll know in a moment, this is the Arcade.
Listen! Hear carolling and songs of good cheer.
Our Minstrels are favorites this time of year.
Santa's here and he looks just fine.
He's taken up residence at 6th and Pine.
The children are waiting, their eyes all aglow,
to give him their list, and hope for snow.
If shopping with little ones leaves you undone:
Stop by our nursery, where they're sure to have fun.
In a hurry, no time to lose.
Can't decide just what to choose.
Then this is the place for 'Gifts to Go'.
All of them wrapped and tied with a bow.
Come see our stores, come share the fun.
It's Christmas everywhere, downtown,
Southcenter, Aurora, and Bellevue Square!
And so to our friends, both old and new,
we want you to know, Christmas isn't Christmas
without a visit from YOU!

Aunt Jo with Carol

The Bon Marché
Seattle

34

Christmas Traditions Growing Up

My family celebrated Christmas in many locations while my father was a pilot in the United States Navy. On Guam, Christmas trees were shipped in from the "states". In Newfoundland we walked into the woods and cut down a tree. The Christmas tree, Christmas stockings, candlelight service with Christmas Carols sung, the making of the many Christmas cookies and treats were all necessary traditions that my family enjoyed. There were Christmas plays that each one of us participated in. There were many decorations around town that we enjoyed caravanning to at night, especially if it included a Christmas Tree Lane. We enjoyed singing around the piano, stereo, or tape deck. There were Christmas stories, especially with the New Testament's one of the Christ Child being born in Bethlehem, long ago. This story my dad enjoyed reading (sometimes every version) to us every Christmas evening before the opening of one present. The rest saved for the morning (if we could wait that long). The morning's breakfast always included Ugnspannkaka or the famous "Dutch Baby", that we knew it to be called, with fruit and amazing toppings. Mid-afternoon there would be an amazing dinner often shared with guests. After this most filling meal we might take a walk around the neighborhood to enjoy lawns with many decorations or to wave at neighbors that we might see.

CR

Christmas Traditions Growing Up

We celebrated Christmas on Christmas Eve, Julaften. When I was young and lived in Huntington, Long Island, we went to a Norwegian Lutheran Church. We would sing Norwegian Christmas songs while circling around the big Christmas tree holding hands. Everything was in Norwegian, which was very unusual after the 1950s. We ate Cod fish, potatoes with melted butter, pearl onions and lingonberries. For dessert, we had "Riskren" or rice pudding with a red sauce. Inside the pudding was a hidden nut and whomever had it got a chocolate or marzipan pig called a "gris". Presents were opened after dinner. Then Christmas Day was a great roast beef dinner after attending a local church service. We all spoke Norwegian daily, especially when my mom's parents, my Nana and Grandpa, were over. (However, not my 4 younger brothers.) I continued this tradition with my son, so he knows fluent Norwegian, too. My grandma, Nana, lived until she was 95, so my son was able to get to know her. They had a very special relationship. She is missed greatly. If I could only be half as good a person as she was.

LD

In Norway, Christmas begins on the 23rd of December, Lille Julaften, Little Christmas Eve. There is a "big house clean", and the making of gingerbread houses. The tree, a real Norway Spruce, is usually decorated by the whole household.

After this there is a tradition to hide mops and brooms
to prevent trolls (or witches) from taking them and flying through
the sky. Also on the 24th of December, a Christmas sheaf,
Julenek is hung from trees or polls for the birds.

Christmas Eve, the 24th, windows are often decorated
with stars, advent lights, with an advent wreath close by. Gifts are
opened after dinner. The evening is a celebration with traditional cookies and cakes. Of course there's Julebrus (a raspberry
Christmas Soda made from blackcurrant juice for the kids and
Glogg, a spiced mulled wine, for the older individuals. Christmas
Day goes something like this: A bountiful breakfast, followed
by a trip to the nearest church for the celebration, Carols sung
with hands held around a Christmas Tree, as church bells ring.
Preparations have been made far in advance with the lamb, ham or
roast wrapped carefully. The burning birch twigs in the fireplace
giving off a wonderful smell to start the meal. Lefse, lutefisk, Nettle
soup, rutabaga mash, salmon, on and on to the abundance on the
table. The prayer is said before beginning. There are wonderful
things including rice cream pudding with red sauce for dessert.
The person getting an almond in their pudding gets a marzipan
chocolate pig. "The Journey to the Christmas Star" is often
watched initiating a visit from Julenisse, Santa, with more gifts,
especially for the children.

Norwegian Table Prayer

I Jesu navn går vi til bords,
å spise og drikke på ditt ord.
Deg, Gud, til ære, oss til gavn.
Så får vi mat i Jesu navn.
Amen

Norwegian American Cousins Remember

Holiday Desserts

Ingen roser uten torner
No roses without thorns

Chapter 2

LD

Kransekake

Butter Cookie Almond Wreath Cake
(Using the traditional Wreath Cake Rings)

I cup (2 sticks unsalted) butter at room temperature
I cup almond paste, also at room temperature
2-1/2 c. all purpose four
I cup powdered sugar
I t. almond extract
2 egg yokes

Cream together the butter, almond paste, and sugar until very
smooth. Blend in the almond extract and egg yolks. In a separate bowl, stir together the salt and the four, and then blend this
into the butter mixture. Chill the dough tor 30 minutes.
350 degrees for 20 minutes, testing with toothpick.
Ice with powder sugar icing.

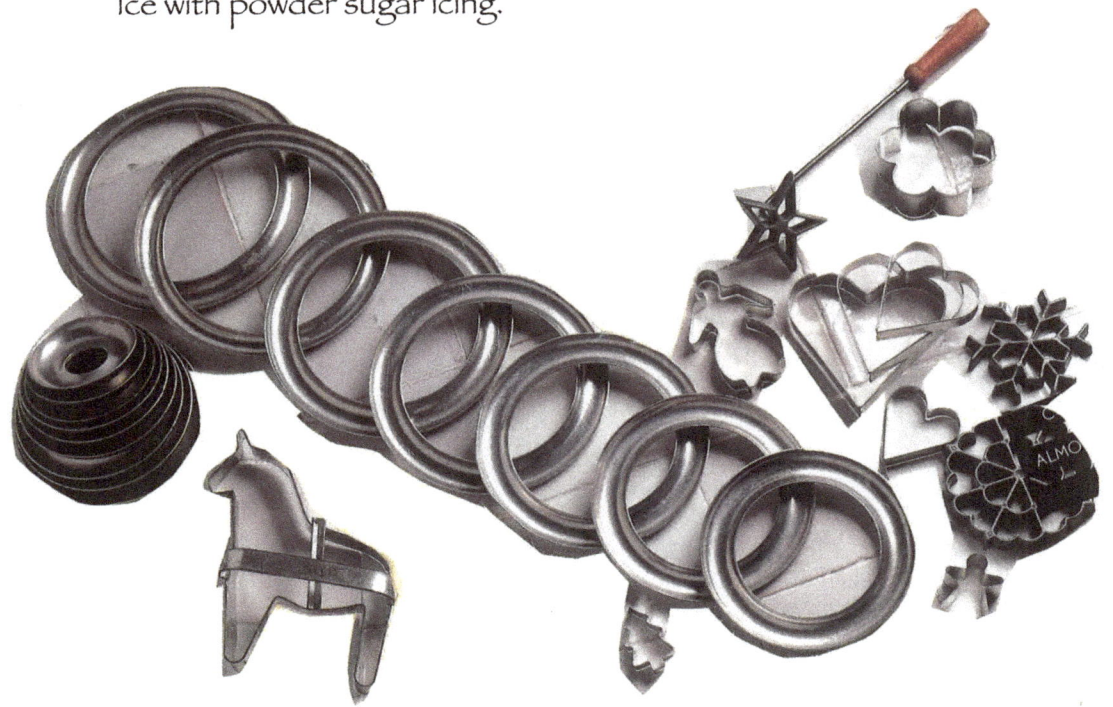

Christmas was a special treat in Norwegian-American homes. There were so many cookies and cakes made. Some of my favorites were Berlinerkranser, Krumkaker, and Sandkaker. We each had our favorites. I remember my grandfather's favorite was Kafekake, coffeecake with raisins. My grandmother's favorite was risgot, with a wonderful red sauce. My traditional Norwegian Christmas Dinner as a young girl was cod fish and potatoes with melted butter, pearl onions, carrots, and lingonberry sauce. Ever hear of boiled cod? Very popular in Southern Norway, as was/is the traditional Lutefisk, served at many festivals.

LD

Berliner Kranser

4 Eggs	1/2 Cup Sugar
1 Cup Butter	2-3/4 Cups Flour

Boil 2 of the eggs. Then mash 2 of the egg yolks. Add the sugar and butter. Mix together the sugar, butter and flour. You can put mixture into a cookie press and shape into wreaths. Brush the wreaths with egg whites and sugar. Bake at 375 degrees until light brown.

TANTE CLARA'S BERLINER KRANSER

Ingredients:

4 cups flour   1 cup sugar

3 sticks butter   2 egg yolks / 2 egg whites

Preheat to 350-degree F.

1. Beat egg yolks and sugar together, beat in butter.

2. Work in flour gradually until all even.

3. Roll out in thin strips and form into a crossed ring.

4. Beat the 2 egg whites and brush onto top.

5. Sprinkle with sugar or Pearl sugar.

Place on cookie tray with parchment paper.

Use middle rack in oven

Bake about 9 minutes

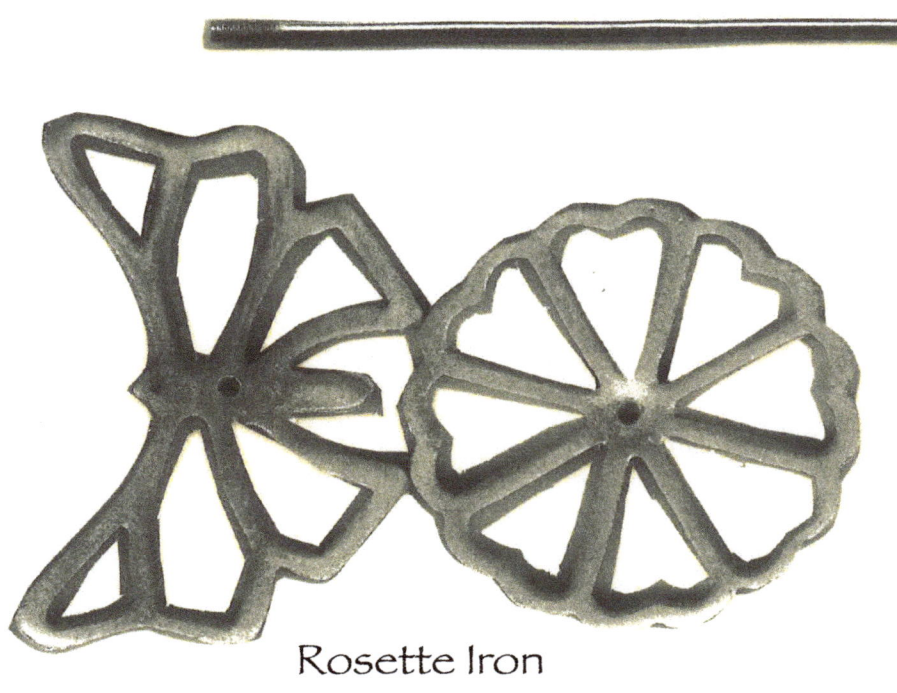

Rosette Iron

Make crisp delicate pastries at home.

Rosettes

Salad oil
1 C. flour
1 C. milk
2 eggs

1 T. vanilla
2 t. sugar
1/4 t. salt

Heat salad oil in skillet to 370 degrees F.
In bowl, beat remaining ingredients until smooth.
Heat Rosette Iron in hot oil and drain. Dip hot
iron into batter to cover 1/4 of form. Return to
hot oil and fry until rosette comes off iron and
turns golden brown. Remove with slotted spoon
and drain, leaving iron in hot oil. Repeat.
Sprinkle with confectioners sugar and enjoy.

Nisse, trickster

 # RIS KREM
Cream of Rice

3/4 cup white rice (not minute rice)
1/2 cup sugar
1 qt. milk
1 tsp. salt
1 almond - whole

2 cups heavy cream, whipped
and sweetened to taste
1/2 cup almonds
1 tsp. almond extract

(serves 8)

Cook rice, salt, and milk in double boiler until rice is soft and mixture is thick, about 1-1/2 hours. Add sugar and almond extract. Chill. Add chopped almonds and 1 whole one. Stir in whipped cream. Serve with Red Fruit Sauce.

RED FRUIT SAUCE

2 cups fruit juice of your choice: currant, strawberry, or raspberry
2 Tbs. potato flour
Sugar if needed
Cold water

Bring juice to a boil. Dissolve potato flour with a little water. Remove juice from heat and slowly add the potato flour thickening, stirring constantly to assure its smoothness. Bring quickly to boil and remove from heat. The sauce should be smooth and not too thick. Pour into container and sprinkle a little sugar over the top to prevent film from forming. Chill. Makes 2 cups.

KRUMKAKER

(pre-heat Krumkaker iron)

CREAM: 1 CUP butter or margarine (or 1/2 + 1/2)

                 1 CUP sugar

                 1-1/2 cups four

ADD: 4 eggs

ADD: 1 t. vanilla

                 1 t. ground cardamon

MIX WELL Drop about 1 T. on Krumkaker iron. (low heat) Bake on both sides until golden, then rolling with the cone shaped pin. The cones can be Riled with cream, or whipped cream, ice cream and berries. Recipe makes about 60 cookie cones.

Krumkaker seems to be loved by most everyone and could be the first dessert to disappear at an event. Carol, Christy's mom, in her later years made Krumkaker for gifts at Christmas, Birthdays, and special holidays.

"I like to think this was even a 'ministry' of hers as she gave plates of Krumkaker to friends, families at church and family get-togethers".

CR

"My mom, Alice, made Krumkaker as gifts and I carry on her tradition."

LD

Mom's Best Crispy Norwegian Oatmeal Cookies
Havrekjekks

1 tsp. baking powder	2 cups granulated sugar
1 lb. unsalted butter	1/2 cup light brown sugar
2 large eggs	2 cups flour

3 cups Old Fashioned Rolled Oats

Preheat oven to 350 degrees. Adjust oven rack to middle position. Line baking sheets with parchment paper.

1. In a medium bowl, combine butter-softened and sugar. (2 cups white, 1/4 cup light brown sugar,) Beat together Increasing speed until light and fluffy.
2. Add eggs to sugar and butter mixture and beat.
3. Add flour mixture to large bowl with above mixture.
4. Gradually add the oatmeal mixture until well combined.
5. Scoop out 1 T.-sized mounds of dough and roll to form balls.
6. Place on cookie sheet (about 16 scoops on sheet)
7. Bake until golden brown on edges, about 10 minutes.

Cooling the cookies on the baking sheet will yield crisper, more perfect cookies.

This is from my mom's old recipe with a few changes.

LD

SANDKAKER

3/4 Cup + 2 T. butter
1/2 Cup almonds (blanched and ground)
1/2 Cup sugar
1/4 t. almond extract

Cup + 1-1/2 T. flour
1 Egg
1/4 t. vanilla

Cream butter and sugar until light and fluffy. Add ground almonds, egg, and vanilla and stir. Add flour and salt. Work ingredients together with your hands. Let dough rest for an hour in refrigerator. Press into greased Sandkake forms. Bake at 375 degrees.

Debbie Erdevig Schleifer

Debbie's family always served Aebleskivers
Christmas morning served with Cardamon and jam.
Debbie's ancestor is Thomas Hansen Erdevig.

Aebleskiver
Nordic Pancake Balls

1 Cup flour

1/2 tsp. baking soda

1-3/4 cup buttermilk

3 eggs

1/4 tsp. salt

1 Tbsp. vanilla sugar

3-1/2 oz. butter

1 Tbsp. sugar

1. Separate egg whites and yolks
2. Whisk sugar and egg whites until fluffy and stiff.
3. Mix the egg yolks, flour and baking soda
   (salt and vanilla sugar in a separate bowl)
4. Use hand mixer while gradually adding buttermilk
5. Melt butter-let cool- to slowly add to buttermilk while whisking
6. Use wooden spoon to slowly mix stiff egg whites into batter.

Heat up special 6 holed pan on burner, butter each hole, filling batter 3/4 full in each. When golden turn over. At this time you can add different fillings. (even apple or jam or chocolate chip)

Aebleskiver means apple pancake even though no apples are in the recipe. You can of course add them. Also, I believe this recipe originated from the Danish.

My granddaughter Gwyneth (below), and my daughter Christina (right), are showing their excitement over this delicious "Dutch Baby" just straight out of the oven. Our whole family shares this enthusiasm, as well, each time it is made. My mother Carol (page 20) is showing off her talent and love for the same.

CA

Topping for Ugnspannkaka
(Dutch Baby)

1/2 cup Berries - fresh or frozen (blueberries, raspberries, and blackberries)

1 T. lemon juice

1 T. butter

1 T. honey

1/2 teaspoon lemon extract

In a small saucepan, melt butter over low-heat and stir in berries. Stir in lemon juice, honey and lemon extract. Stir regularly and keep very low. Serve hot by ladling sauce over "pancake."

Many cultures have a breakfast meal similar to Ugnspannkaka, the Nordic/Norwegian oven pancake. The German pancake version is called Dutch Baby. That is what my family has called it for many celebrations, especially on Christmas morning. If you consider the ingredients of : eggs, flour, milk and melted butter, then we could say many have a similar breakfast meal. Take for example:

Americans have pancakes.
The French have Le Crepe.
Swedish call it pannkakor. (may be with bacon)
England's version is similar to Yorkshire Pudding.
African pancake is like a spongy crepe.

In any country these versions make breakfast even more delicious by adding toppings like ....

fruit, sour cream, powdered sugar,
lemon butter, or even vegetables.

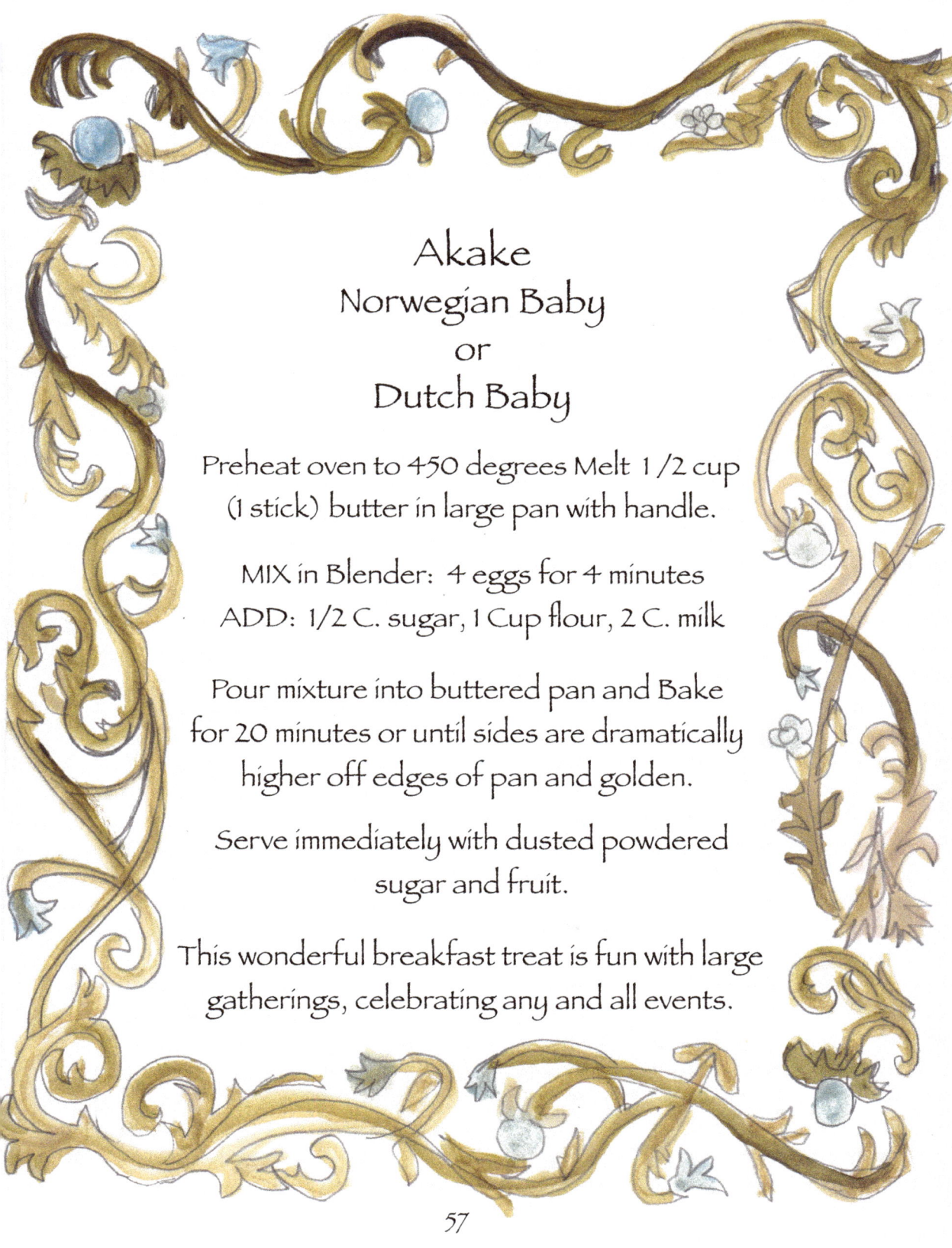

Akake
Norwegian Baby
or
Dutch Baby

Preheat oven to 450 degrees Melt 1/2 cup
(1 stick) butter in large pan with handle.

MIX in Blender: 4 eggs for 4 minutes
ADD: 1/2 C. sugar, 1 Cup flour, 2 C. milk

Pour mixture into buttered pan and Bake
for 20 minutes or until sides are dramatically
higher off edges of pan and golden.

Serve immediately with dusted powdered
sugar and fruit.

This wonderful breakfast treat is fun with large
gatherings, celebrating any and all events.

Fattigmann

Fattigmann cookies are traditional Christmas cookies in Norway. Some say these cookies got the name "poor man's cookies" because they were the only cookies the less fortunate could afford to make around the holidays. Another version of why they were called that was that they were said to leave the baker "in the poor house". They are considered very special and a part of the Christmas celebration.

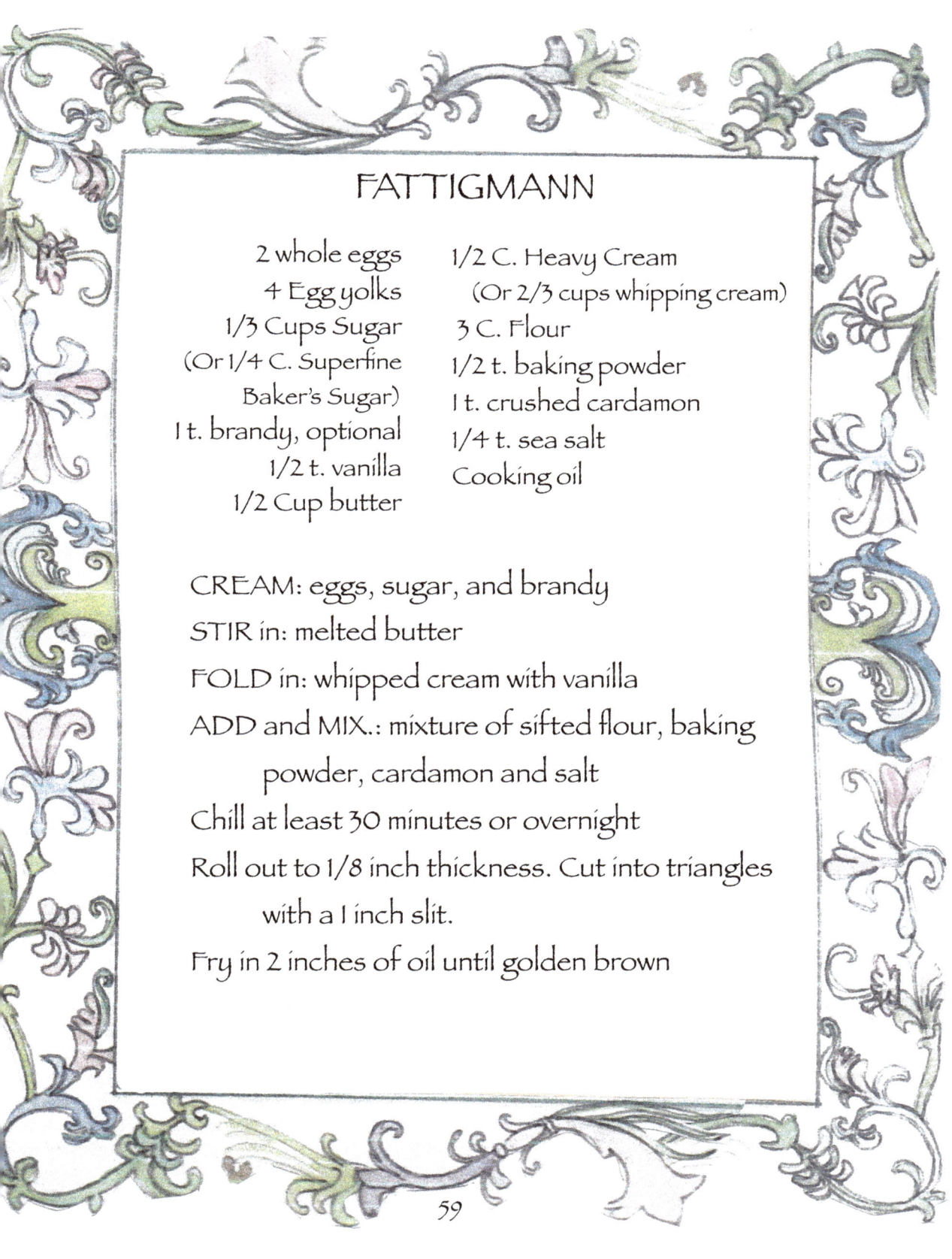

FATTIGMANN

2 whole eggs
4 Egg yolks
1/3 Cups Sugar
(Or 1/4 C. Superfine
Baker's Sugar)
1 t. brandy, optional
1/2 t. vanilla
1/2 Cup butter

1/2 C. Heavy Cream
   (Or 2/3 cups whipping cream)
3 C. Flour
1/2 t. baking powder
1 t. crushed cardamon
1/4 t. sea salt
Cooking oil

CREAM: eggs, sugar, and brandy

STIR in: melted butter

FOLD in: whipped cream with vanilla

ADD and MIX.: mixture of sifted flour, baking
   powder, cardamon and salt

Chill at least 30 minutes or overnight

Roll out to 1/8 inch thickness. Cut into triangles
   with a 1 inch slit.

Fry in 2 inches of oil until golden brown

Serina Kaker
Linda's Great Aunt Clara's Recipe

3-1/2 cups of flour   2eggs

1 cup sugar   1 teaspoon baking powder

3 sticks butter   1 teaspoon vanilla

Mix flour, sugar, baking powder, vanilla, and 1 egg.
Cut in butter and cream until smooth.
Roll into small balls and put on baking sheet and flatten with fork.
Beat 1 egg, brush on cookies, and sprinkle with chopped almonds and sugar.
Bake at 350 degrees.

Norwegian Gingerbread Cookies
Pepperkaker

1/2 lb. unsalted 'butter

1/4 unsulphured molasses

  (or lys syrup-Norway

1 cup Powered Sugar

3.4 oz. Heavy cream (if you want)

2 large eggs

1 cup dark brown sugar

3 cups Sifted All-purpose flour

2 tsp. ground ginger

2 tsp. ground cinnamon

1-1/2 tsp. ground cloves

2 tsp. nutmeg

1 tsp. ground pepper

1/2 tsp. salt

2 tsp. baking soda

1/2 tsp. baking powder

Supposedly single women should eat these cookies
to increase their chances of getting a good man.

Melt butter, syrup, heavy cream and powdered sugar in
saucepan. Let this cool before adding other ingredients.
Mix well. Knead. Cool over night.

Pre-heat oven to 350 degrees
Roll out dough between 2 sheets of parchment
Cut out desired shapes
Bake for 10 minutes

JULEKAKA
Classic Norwegian Christmas bread, laced with cardamom and studded with candied fruits and raisin. Available standard for $10.5 or garnished w/icing & candied fruit for $11. $10.5 / 11

There is a Byen Bakery on 15 Nickerson Seattle, Washington that my daughters, grandkids, and I love to visit. On my daughter Beth's birthday, her family buys her the famous Princess Cake. The Julekaka, shown above, can have fruit or nuts in it. Both versions are delicious.

JULEKAKA

1 cup raisins
2 tbsp. Sherry , Port or Vin Santo
1 stick plus 1 tbsp. butter
1-1/4 cups milk
1 tbsp. fresh yeast (or 2 tsp instant)
4 cups strong bread flour
1/3 cup caster sugar
2 tsp. fine salt
2 tsp. ground cardamon seeds
2 tbsp. orange peel, chopped
1 beaten egg (for glazing)
Pearl sugar tor sprinkling/ dusting

Soak the raisins in the liquor heated to boiling. Melt the butter and add to milk. Crumble in yeast for 15 minutes-to foam up. Add flour, sugar, salt, and the cardamon. Knead by hand or in a standing mixer. (with dough hook: Knead until smooth , stretchy, and stops sticking. Drain the raisins and add to dough with peel. Mix gently. Place dough in a bowl in warm area to double. (takes about an hour) Turn onto floured surface and shape into round loaf. Place on parchment lined baking sheet=40 min. Preheat oven to 400 F. Brush with beaten egg . Bake in lower half of oven 40 minutes until golden brown.

Norwegian Sweet Soup
(SOT SUPPE)

Ingredients:
5 cups water
1/4 cup large pearl tapioca
1 cup chopped prunes
1/2 cup raisins
1 cup mixed dried fruit, chopped
3/4 cup sugar
1 T. lemon juice

Instructions:
1. Soak the tapioca in water overnight. In the morning, add fruit) sugar, cinnamon) and lemon zest.

2. Cook over medium-high heat in a large) heavy bottomed saucepan until tapioca is clear and the fruit is tender, about 10 minutes. Remove from heat and add lemon juice. Allow to cool. Store in refrigerator tor up to 1 week.

FRUIT SOUP

CUT: 1 cup apricots and 1 cup peaches, apples and or prunes (my cousin used rhubarb) 3/4 cup sugar and lemon zest. Put into 2-1/2 quart saucepan with 5 cups water.

ADD: golden and dark raisins, currants, cinnamon stick, orange peel and 1/4 cup large pearl tapioca.

LET STAND for 1 hour. (some let tapioca soak overnight, then add rest)

COOK: over medium heat until dear tapioca and fruit is tender. (30 min)

Remove from heat and add 1 Tablespoon lemon juice. Serve with a dollop of cream.

My grandmother Harda Erdevig would make Fruit Soup for special occasions. I chose to make and bring it to an International University Pot-Luck Dinner where my daughter Christina attended in pre-school.

Rabarbrasuppe

1/2 lb, pink and green rhubarb, chopped
(about 2 cups)
2 cups water
6 T. sugar
1 T. red wine vinegar
1 t. vanilla
1 T. cornstarch mixed in 1/4 cup water

In a heavy bottomed pot add rhubarb
Bring to boil, simmer 25 minutes
Heat adding the cornstarch mix
Chill in the frig until ready to serve
Top with cream/milk + sugar/cinnamon

For a smoother texture puree rhubarb

The only Fruit Soup that was made by our Lillesand family was
Rabarrbra Suppe, Rhubarb Soup, and I loved it. However, no
one could make it back in the United States, that I knew of. I
even tried to make it, but the rhubarbs that I would buy here
were always so bitter. In Norway, the rhubarbs were so sweet.

LD

Prune Pudding
or
SVISKER GROT

1/2 lb. prunes	1/8 t. salt
2 cups water just below boiling)	1 T. lemon juice
1 cup sugar	1 cup corn starch
1 inch cinnamon stick	1/2 cup boiling water

1. Wash prunes in hot water -simmer with salt
2. Remove stones and add sugar, salt, cinnamon simmer for 10 minutes
3. Make paste with corn starch and cold water add to prune mixture and cook tor 5 minutes.
4. Remove cinnamon
5. Add lemon juice
6. Pour into mold -Chill-serve with cream

Variation:
Fold in stiffly beaten whites of 2 eggs + (2 T. sugar)
Can also add 1/2 cup of nuts.

Norwegian-English Table Prayer

In Jesus name we go to the table
to eat and drink according to your word.
To God, the honor, to us, the gain.
So, we have food, in Jesus name.
Amen

Norwegian American Cousins Remember

Traditional Recipes

jo flere kokker jo mer søl
The more cooks, the more mess

Chapter 3

Lobster Tails with Compound Butter

You might want to pick out a fresh lobster to begin with. And
the method that you want to cook your fresh lobster; Steaming,
baking, broiling and grilling are a few ways. Norwegian Lobsters
have a light orange color similar to shrimp. As a food, the Norway
lobster is smaller than Maine lobster, is similar to crab taste and
texture, and is sweeter than shrimp. Which ever kind of lobster you
use your end result will most likely be delicious.

To broil your lobster:
Heat your broiler to high. Put a cooling rack in a half sheet pan.
Halve the lobster tails. Cut the tails in half lengthwise and place
on rack cut side up. Spread the compound butter on each 1/2 of a
lobster tail. (2 teaspoons at this time).

To make a compound butter to spread on the lobsters you'll need:
4~8 oz. butter (or even 2 sticks of) unsalted butter
1/4 cup chopped chives   1 T. chopped fresh parsley
chopped shallots   Zest of lemon
2 T. chopped fresh tarragon   Fresh ground pepper

Broil the lobster(s) until the lobster meat is white and opaque and
the shell is red. (4 minutes usually).
Serve the lobsters with more compound butter and serve.

Maine Lobster

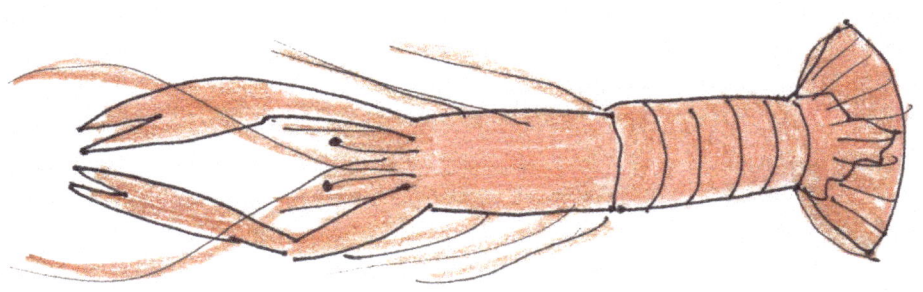

Norwegian Lobster

LINDA'S TURKEY
(Black Pepper and Maple Roast Turkey)

How to Safely Thaw a Turkey

Be sure to let your turkey completely thaw before cooking. If it was frozen through when you bought it, the turkey will thaw within a few days in the fridge, approximately 24 hours for every five pounds of turkey. For quicker thawing, place the turkey in a cold water bath (it is not safe to thaw a turkey with warm water) and change the water every 30 minutes until it's thawed - about a half hour per pound.

The simplest and safest way to thaw a whole frozen turkey is in the refrigerator. It will need 24 hours for every 5 pounds of turkey.

Preheat at 450 degrees and when ready to put turkey in oven, then lower temp to 350 degrees. Put the roasting pan in the lower third of the oven and remove racks above. Place some crumpled up sheets of aluminum foil and place in the bottom of the disposable roasting pan (if you don't have a roasting rack).

Place the butter, 1 tablespoon of the maple syrup, 1 ½ tsp pepper, and 1 tsp salt in a small bowl and smash together with a spoon or rubber spatula until combined; set aside. Make in advance and store in refrigerator up to 2 days.

Remove the neck and giblets. Pat the cavity and the outside of the turkey dry with paper towels and place breast-side up on a cutting board. Loosen the skin on the breast and the legs by gently sliding your hand between the meat and the skin and separating it without tearing it. Distribute the butter evenly under the loosened skin. Season the outside and cavity of the turkey generously with salt and pepper.

Place the turkey breast-side up on the roasting rack/pan. Tie the legs together with kitchen twine if desired. Pour the broth into the roasting pan (2 cups low sodium chicken or turkey broth).

Place the roasting pan in the oven. Immediately turn the temperature down to 350 degrees. Roast for 1 ½ hours. Meanwhile, stir the remaining ¼ cup maple syrup and 1 tablespoon soy sauce together in a small bowl and set aside.

After 1 ½ hours, brush the turkey with the reserved maple syrup mixture every 20 minutes.

Start checking the temperature after 2 hours total roasting time. The turkey is ready when a meat thermometer inserted into the thickest part of the thigh not touching bone registers at least 165 degrees (which should be about 2 ½ to 3 ½ hours total cooking time). It is about 13 minutes per pound.

When the turkey is ready, place the roasting pan on the stove. Lift the neck end of the turkey up at an angle with a wadded-up paper towel so that the juices in the cavity pour out into the roasting pan. Transfer the turkey to a clean cutting board or serving platter and let rest at least 30 minutes before carving. Meanwhile, remove the roasting rack, if any, and make the gravy.

Fit a fine-mesh strainer over a heat proof medium bowl. Using a wooden spoon, scrape up any browned bits from the bottom of the roasting pan. Pour the pan juices through the strainer and discard the contents of the strainer. Set aside for a few minutes for the fat to rise to the surface.

Spoon off ¼ cup of the fat from the surface of the pan juices into a medium saucepan (if you don't have enough fat, add oil or butter as needed to get to ¼ cup). Spoon off and discard the remaining fat. Measure the remaining juices, known as drippings and add broth as needed to get to 2 ½ cups (if you have more than 2 ½ cups of drippings already, that's fine); set aside.

Place the saucepan over medium-high heat until the fat is shimmering. Whisk in the flour and cook until slightly darkened in color, about 1 minute. Pour in the reserved pan juices, whisk to combine, and bring to a simmer. Simmer until thickened to desired consistency. Taste and season with soy sauce (1 teaspoon at a time), salt, and more coarsely ground pepper as needed.

Recipe for Compound Butter

1. 8 Tbsp/1 stick unsalted butter, softened   2. ¼ cup maple syrup and 1 tablespoon maple syrup (divided)   3. 1½ tsp black pepper, coarse   4. 1 tsp salt

Mix and use this to spread under the skin of the turkey, being careful not to break through the skin. Separate the skin by using your hand to get between the meat of the breast and the legs. Rub the compound butter between the meat and the skin.

Rullepolse

Cousin Josie makes Rullepolse at Christmas time. After rolling she will put the pork in brine for two weeks, then put it in a large pot to boil (with peppercorns, cloves, bay leaves, etc.). Then simmer for an hour or two. You can refrigerate for 12 hours then slice and eat.

Sage Breaded Dressing/Stuffing

1 -1/2 cups chopped celery with leaves
3/4 cup finely chopped onion
3/4 cup butter
9 cups soft bread crumbs

1 t. salt
1/2 t. ground sage
1/2 t. dried thyme leaves
1/4 t. pepper

Cook and stir celery and onion in butter in Dutch oven until celery is tender: remove from heat. Stir in remaining ingredients.
Makes 5 cups stuffing: 410 calories per cup.
I think was an Erdevig favorite!

Variations: Apple-Raisin, Cornbread, Mushroom, Oyster, Sausage and Giblet Stuffing.

Cousin Josie

Josie and her mom Edna use to make Sage Dressing together.
This was something Christy's mom Carol, and grandmother Harda, loved doing together too.

FISH CAKES

18 oz. Fresh Norwegian Cod
3/4 cup whole milk or extra creamy oat milk
4 T. Butter or avocado oil, for frying
3 T. Potato starch

3/4 t. Sea salt
1/2 t. ground nutmeg
1/2 t. Black pepper

Directions:

Pat the fish dry to remove all excess moisture. Add the fish to the bowl of a food processor or blender. With the processor or motor running, slowly stream in the milk, followed by the salt, spices, and starch. Process 2 minutes until smooth and a thick mixture is achieved.

Dip a large spoon in warm water and scoop out large spoonfuls of the fish mixture into 16 equal round discs and fatten slightly. Heat a large (non-stick) fry pan over a medium high heat. Fry 4 fish cakes at a time with 1 tablespoon of butter or oil tor each batch. Cook for about 4 minutes per side, and until golden brown on both sides. When fully cooked through, the fish cakes should be firm to the touch.
Serve with tartar sauce.

Lapskaus
(Beef and Vegetable Stew)

900 g / 2 lbs Beef (Stew quality)

1 pcs Big onion

600 g / 1-1/3 lbs Potatoes

5 pcs Carrots

1/2 pcs Celery Root

1 pcs Small Rutabaga (or Turnip)

1-1/3 c. Beef Stock

1 T. Olive Oil

2 T. Butter

3 T. Flour

2 pcs Bay Leaves

4 pcs Thyme Stems

Salt and Pepper

Fresh Parsley

1/4 c. Red Wine

1. Cut the meat in small pieces

2. Chop the vegetables in small pieces

3. Heat 1 T. butter and the olive oil

4. Heat the remaining butter in the stew pan to fry onions

5. Add the meat, and flour and mix well

6. Add the vegetables

7. Add beef stock and wine, little by little

8. Add bay leaves and thyme

9. Continue to cook until stew thickens

ENJOY!

Norwegian Potato Dumplings
(Raspeball)

2-1/4 lb. Shredded raw potatoes

Heaping 3 cups potatoes, peeled,

cooked, mashed, then cooled

1-1/4 cup barley four

2 tsp. salt

Directions:

1. Mix the shredded raw potatoes with the cold boiled mashed potatoes.

2. Add the barley four and 1 teaspoon of the salt and mix.

3. Put on large saucepan of water to boil and add 1 teaspoon salt

4. Form a round ball by using a tablespoon and your hand.

5. Place raspeballer gentler into soft boiling water and let them simmer tor about 45 minutes.

6. Serve the dumplings immediately.

Norwegian Komper

Komper are wintry orange-sized, slow-simmered dumplings made of grated potato and barley flour and often filled with pork. They are quite popular through-out Norway. The great thing about Komper is that they taste even greater the day after.

Mix:

2 cups of flour 1/2 t. salt, 1/4 t. baking powder, 1/4 t. pepper. Place in a large bowl: 4 cups grated and peeled potatoes and 2 T. grated Red Onion and combine with the flour mixture and the potato's juice. Form orange-size ball and shape around a cube of pork pieces. Drop into large pot of boiling water with 2 t. salt and simmer for 45min. Drain and serve with peas or beets. The next day the Komper can be fried in butter with eggs for breakfast!

Some of my happiest memories while young was coming home to the smell of my mom's cooking, Komper. These are something like potato balls with pork (flesk) inside. The potatoes were wrapped and mixed with corn flakes and oatmeal, then formed into large balls with a little salted pork inside. They were then boiled in a large pot. They were served with different things for dinner; maple syrup, lingonberries, melted butter, etc., depending on the mood. The BEST, however, was the next day's left-overs!!! The Kompers were sliced up, fried, and served for breakfast with sugar or syrup on top.

LD

My Early Years with Lefse

When I was in 2nd grade my class was learning about the first Native Americans and their culture. I helped paint a mural about them. We also learned of their delicious Frybread, a basically flatter bread than that made with yeast. I heard the word "flat" and immediately volunteered to have my grandmother make some for the whole class. Turns out that lefse, a Norwegian flat bread, is not Native American. However, I didn't know that at the time. Sure enough, my grandmother made lefse for the whole class. However, when my teacher, Ms. Stephens called to thank my grandmother for the Native American flatbread, she was kind of upset that I had confused lefse with Frybread. However, both are delicious, yet very different.

CR

Lefse

Edna's Recipe

5 large potatoes
3 tbs butter
½ cup sweet cream
1 teas salt
Flour - ½ cup to each cup of mashed potatoes

Cook potatoes, and then rice or mash them. Add other
ingredients. Roll out on floured board and cut in circles.
Grandma Edna used a bread plate.
Bake on electric grill or fry pan about 450.

From Josie Lehde, daughter of Edna

The history of lutefisk dates back to the Vikings. On one occasion, according to one legend, plundering Vikings burned down a fishing village, including the wooden racks with drying cod. The returning villagers poured water on the racks to put out the fire. Ashes covered the dried fish, and then it rained. The fish buried in the ashes thus became soaked in lye slush. Later the villagers were surprised to see that the dyed fish had changed to what looked like fresh fish. They rinsed the fish in water to remove the lye and make it edible and then boiled it. The story is that one particular brave villager tasted the fish and declared it "not bad".

I have read that one can either love lutefisk or hate it and that some people say , "once a year is enough!" One relative of mine loves it. While it isn't exactly my favorite, wrapped in lefse it's good. In Norway, it is served on special days and traditional holidays. You can find it at an Norwegian-American deli and certainly within communities at Thanksgiving and Christmastime. Usually , lutefisk, after boiling or baking, adding butter, salt, and pepper has the consistency of jello or very soft scrabbled eggs.

I have heard it told that Norwegian-Americans believe that lutefisk was brought by their ancestors on the ships when they came to America, and that it was all they had to eat. The fish is celebrated anyway and linked with hardship and courage.

Lutefisk

You can purchase lutefisk trimmed and packaged in a plastic bag. Plan on getting this a day before you plan on serving it. Take it out of the plastic bag, put in a large bowl, and cover with ice water. Change the water two to three times to remove any lye, and keep in the refrigerator until ready to use. This firms up the fish. Cook in boiling pot of water, or in the oven at 400 degrees. You can "soak" in butter, add salt and pepper or cinnamon and sugar. Roll up in lefse. Or cut into pieces and coat in a beer batter and deep fry. Eat while hot. Serve with bacon, potatoes, and lefse.

CR

KILL IT: LUTEFISK
—Author unknown,
Le Mesnagier de Paris, circa 1393

- A Bit of Humor -
found in an old Seattle book shop

Nettle Tea

To make Nettle Tea, pour 1 cup of boiling water over 3-4 tsp. of dried nettle leaves. Steep, covered tor 10 minutes, then sweeten with honey. For best results sip the tea halt an hour after meals. It is a perfect thirst quencher.

It also provides many health benefits because nettles are rich in vitamins and minerals. Often these stimulating and detoxifying properties combine to produce a fresh clear complexion.

Nettle Star Bread
(with Cheesy Mushroom Filling)

Bread Ingredients:
1 ¾ c. all-purpose flour
¼ c. dried, powdered nettles
1 2 tsp. Yeast
¼ c. potato flour

¾ cup – 1 c. lukewarm milk
¼ c. butter at room temperature
2 tsp. Salt
1 egg – reserve for egg wash

Directions:

1. Sift the flour, nettle powder, potato flour, remaining ingredients and pour in. Knead more milk or flour as needed to adjust the Dough should spring back if you poke it

2. Place the dough into a lightly-greased bowl and cover. Let rise until doubled, about an hour.

3. Divide the dough into 4 even balls and set on a greased baking sheet. Cover and let rest for another 15-20 minutes while you make the filling (below.)

4. On a piece of parchment paper, roll one of the portions of dough into a 10" circle. (It's okay if it's not perfectly round or even.)

5. Spread on ½ of the cooked mushroom mixture, leaving ½" of bare dough around the edge. On top of the mushrooms, sprinkle ½ c. grated Gouda, ½ c. grated Parmesan, 1 Tbs. hemp hearts, and 1 tsp. Nettle seeds.

6. Roll out a second circle the same as the first and place it on top of the first circle. Repeat step 5 with another third of the filling ingredients.

7. Repeat the process with the third circle, then place the fourth circle on top with no toppings on it.

8. Place a 2 ½" round glass in the center of the dough circle to act as a guide. With a sharp knife or kitchen shears, cut the circle into 16 equal strips from the glass to the edge, going through all the layers. (It's easiest to do this by cutting 4 in the shape of a cross, then cutting between each of those, then between those as well.) You should have a wagon-wheel like design.

9. Pick up two adjacent dough strips and twist them away from each other twice so that the top side is facing up again. (I like to hold one strip in each hand and twist them at the same time.) Dab a little water on the end and pinch the ends together to create a petal-like shape. Repeat this process with the remaining strips of dough so that you end up with 8 pairs of strips.

Legg kokte krabbeklor i en gryte.
Hell konjakk over dem varm opp
(men ikke kok)
tenn på og brenn av ti det ikke
er mer konjakk igjen.

Place the "boiling crab" in one pot.
Pour brandy over them with warm heat
(but not boiling yet)
until the brandy is gone.

Quick Norwegian Herring

1 - 1/2 oz-jar pickled cut herring fillets drained
1 cup sour cream
1 cup thinly sliced onion
1 tsp. dried dill
1/8 tsp. pepper
Add together and serve with Hardtack

Knackebrad 1/Hard Tack
3 cups potato water
1 cake yeast
Flour to make soft sponge
(combine: Let rise overnight in warm place)

Next day:
Add: 1 cup shortening
1 T. salt
1/3 cup sweet cream
1 egg yolk
flour to make soft dough
Knead-let rise - roll as thin as possible in corn meal
Cut in rectangles
Bake 350 degrees

King Crab hor d'oeuvre
serves 12

2 (12 oz.) pkgs. refrigerated biscuit dough or putt pastry shells
1 (8oz.) pkg. cream cheese softened
6 oz. crab meat
2 T mayonnaise
2 T grated Parmesan cheese (or 1 c. shredded mozzarella)
1/2 cup shredded Cheddar cheese
2 T thinly sliced green onions
1 t. Worcestershire sauce
1 pinch paprika

Mix all ingredients and put into puff pastry shells.
Cook for 20 minutes

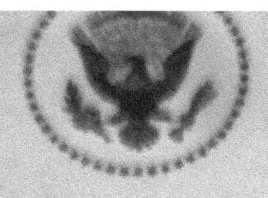

LUNCHEON

Délice of Crabs Mathilda

Almaden
Grenache
Rosé

Tournedos Rossini
Potatoes Berny
Peas à la Française

Piper Heidsieck
1955

Bombe Glacée Josephine

Demi-tasse

The White House
Thursday, May 3, 1962

Blue Crabs = Atlantic Coast
Brown Crabs = Norwegian Coastline
Orange, Red and Purple Crabs =
Puget Sound Coastline
Reddish Brown-Purple Crabs =
West Coast Dungeness

CRAB DIP

12 oz. Cream cheese
2 cloves minced Garlic
3 T. dry White Wine
3 T. Lemon Juice   WHIP
2 t. Dijon Mustard   TOGETHER
1 t. Horseradish
2 t. Worcestershire

1/4 C. Shallots
12 oz. Crab meat   STIR
2 T. Cream   IN
1 C. chopped Artichoke
Salt and Pepper (to taste)

1/2 C. Grated Parmesan Cheese
Heat in 375 Degrees oven   TOP
for 15-20 minutes   WITH

A common ancestor that Christy and I share is Mathilde Heldal, who was cook to the Joseph Kennedy family for over 25 years. She traveled with the family between Hyannis Port and West Palm Beach, but spending her summers in Norway. She was often called back to cook for some special occasions.

Délice of Crabs Mathilda

Legg kokte krabbeklør i en gryte. Hell konjakk over dem, varm opp (men ikke kok), tenn på og brenn av til det ikke er mer konjakk igjen.

I en annen gryte kokes tynn kremfløte under stadig omrøring til den tykner godt, saltes og pepres, tas av varmen og irøres et par eller flere eggeplommer etter porsjonsstørrelsen.

Varm krabbene opp i sausen, ha det hele over i ildfast form og brun kvikt under grillen.

With all due respect to the recipe Crabs Mathilde, I heard that no one can make them as good as she can, using her recipe. So we may want to consider trying to come close.

LD

There was an easy delightful dessert recipe that charmed many of the upper class New York and Boston ladies. These women use to highly compliment Mathilde when she made it for their luncheons. She used to laugh as it was SUCH an EASY, EASY thing to make. It was something like pears from a can and then placed in jello OR in whipped cream and chilled.

LD

Here is a similar version of her recipe that is also so delicious.

Pear Mousse

6 Pears	1/2 t. cinnamon
3/4 oz. Natural Yogurt	1 t. vanilla extract
1/2 pint whipped cream	1 T. powdered sugar
1 Lemon (a few drops)	grated chocolate

1. Whip the cream and powdered sugar until stiff peaks form. Stick in the fridge.
2. Wash and peel the pears with drizzles of lemon. Put pear pieces, vanilla extract, and cinnamon into a blender until pureed.
3. Whisk the pear mixture and the yogurt together. Fold the whipped cream gently in with a spatula.
4. Pour the total "mousse" mixture into 6 bowls and refrigerate for 4 hours. Remove and grate chocolate on top of each.

Norwegian American Cousins Remember

Folktales

Når katten er borte, danser musene på bordet.

When the cat's away the mice dance on the table

Chapter 4

Story Time with Grandma Harda and the Grandkids.

From left to right: Steve, Christy, Harda, Carol, and Linda

Norwegian Folktales are most often associated with Asbjornsen & Moe, storytellers, whose writings appeared in the 1840s until present times. These two met when they were 13 years old and stayed friends, sharing their love for stories. It is said that they collected these stories from the villages and people of rural Norway. The stories seem full of bears, princes and princesses, the sea, giant trolls, talking animals, magic and myths. Sounds quite like that of American Children's Fairy tales. Many are from around the world. Walt Disney Studios has made some of these stories come alive for all to see.

I have summarized these stories that we were read to as children, often until we fell asleep. Then we got to read some to our children and grandchildren. Of course, there are so many more that we have not mentioned, but we wanted to include the ones with Norwegian origin. Also, those read to us by our Norwegian grandmothers.

A Quick Tale To Explain Why the Sea Has Salt

Although there are several versions of this story I will just stick to this version of a poor man who sets out to find more food for his family. He begins with just enough food for himself for his journey. Along the way he meets an old man begging for food. The kind poor man extends such generosity to the old man and shares his food. The old beggar tells him to fetch 2 bowls and to ask for rice. Then they are both off in different directions. So the poor man takes his rice bowls home to his wife. Whatever these bowls are asked to make they are full to overflowing non-stop. A brother of the poor man sees what these bowls can provide and proceeds to steal them. Then he turns and sells them to a sea captain who needs salt for his crew at sea. The bowls produce so much salt that the boat begins to sink. With quick thinking the captain hurls the bowls over the deck of the boat. The bowls are still producing salt for the ocean to this day.

The Three Billy Goats Gruff

Every child has heard the story about the
THREE BILLY GOATS GRUFF.

But I will tell a modified short version here. Once there were 3 goats that had eaten all the green grasses on their side of the river. The only way to get to the other side of the river where green grasses were, was by crossing a bridge. And the trouble was that there lived a troll underneath this bridge. He was a big nasty ugly troll that loved to gobble up billy goats. Little Billy Goat went over first convincing the troll that she was just too little to eat. Then the Middle Billy Goat trip trapped over the bridge telling the troll that their big brother would be the best choice for him. Lastly, Great Big Billy Goat Gruff began his tripping over the bridge with a head on encounter with the TROLL. The Great Big Billy Goat Gruff wasted no time in butting that mean troll into the river below and he was never to be seen there again.

TRIPP TRAPP TRESSKO

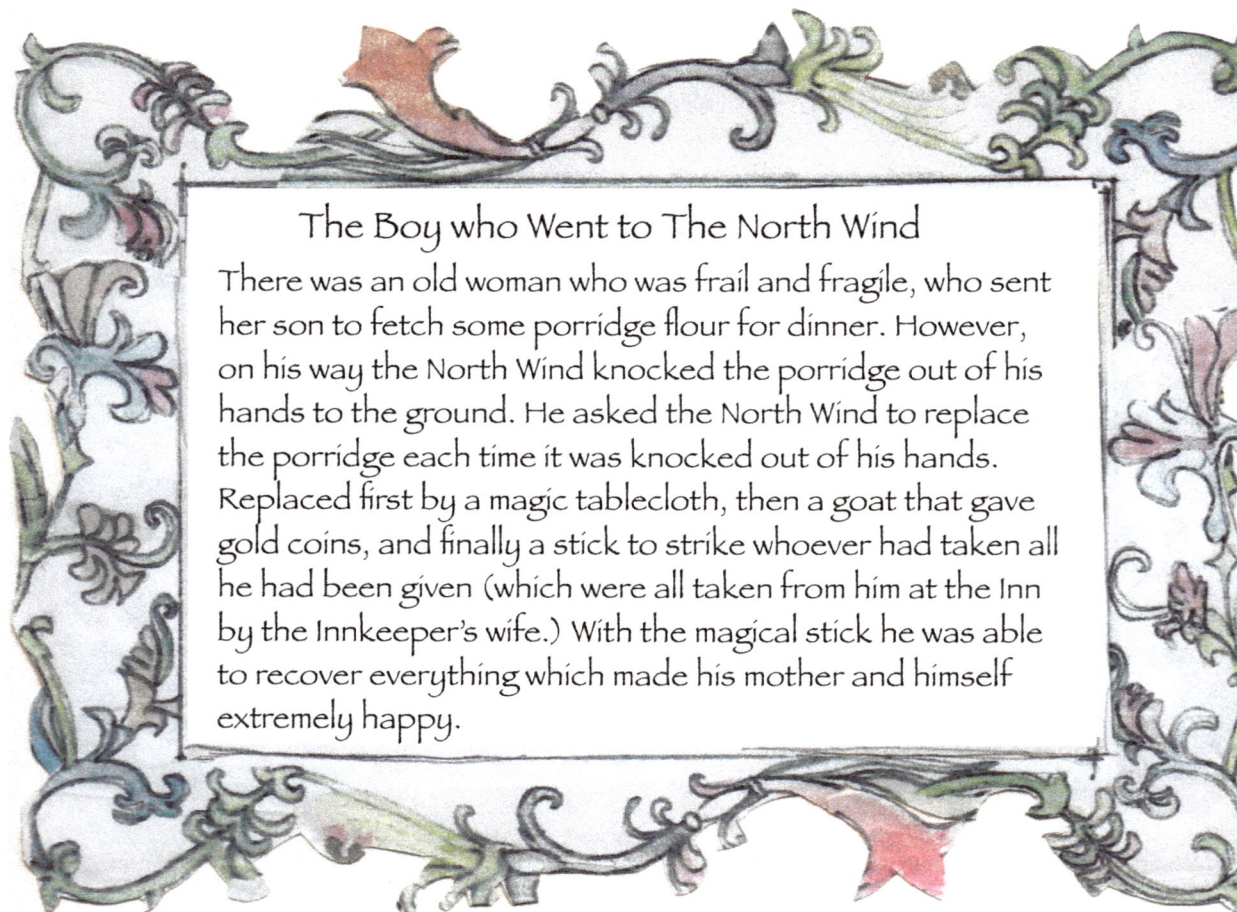

The Boy who Went to The North Wind

There was an old woman who was frail and fragile, who sent her son to fetch some porridge flour for dinner. However, on his way the North Wind knocked the porridge out of his hands to the ground. He asked the North Wind to replace the porridge each time it was knocked out of his hands. Replaced first by a magic tablecloth, then a goat that gave gold coins, and finally a stick to strike whoever had taken all he had been given (which were all taken from him at the Inn by the Innkeeper's wife.) With the magical stick he was able to recover everything which made his mother and himself extremely happy.

Princess On A Glass Hill

Three brothers take turns sleeping in their father's barn at night to see if they can capture the animal who is devouring his lands. Only the third and youngest son, Boots, is able to see, capture, and stop, not only one, but three extraordinary grand horses who were all eating up their father's grassy fields and depleting his barns. Now, of course, king of the country, where Boots lived, had a beautiful daughter. This king said he would give her away to anyone that could climb the glass hill to the castle and able to capture the 3 golden apples she held in her hands. Boot's two brothers tried. And failed. Many other knights and princes would get even 1/2 way up the glass mountain, but would slide down to the bottom, so disappointed. Boots disguised himself with rags over his armor and for the next three days would capture one of the golden apples. The king noticing someone had been able to climb the glass hill and capture the golden apples, called everyone together to find out who. Boots was in the crowd and took off the rags revealing his armor and the 3 golden apples. The king then gladly gave Boots his princess daughter and half of his kingdom!

The White Bear King Valemon

A king had three daughters, one fair and kind. The other two
were the opposite. This daughter longed for a golden wreath
she had seen in her dream. No one was able to duplicate it or
find one that matched it. However, as she was walking in the
forest she saw a white bear playing with the exact golden wreath
she had seen in her dream. She explained her dream to the
bear. She took the wreath with the promise that he could return
for her someday. (This bear was under a spell and was really
King Valemon, but the princess did not know that.) Later he did
return, they married, and lived happily for three years. However
a troll appeared one day and snatched the King away. The
princess was determined to find him and set out on her difficult
journey. People and children saw along the way how kind and
generous she was. At last the spell was broken, the trolls were
scattered, and she found her king. And they lived happily ever
after.

Winken, Blinken, and Nod

Wynken, Blynken, and Nod one night
Sailed off in a wooden shoe —
Sailed on a river of crystal light,
Into a sea of dew.
"Where are you going, and what do
you wish?"
The old moon asked the three.
"We have come to fish for the herring
fish. That live in this beautiful sea;
Nets of silver and gold have we!"
Said Wynken,
Blynken,
And Nod.

The old moon laughed and sang a
song, As they rocked in the wooden
shoe, And the wind that sped them all
night long Ruffled the waves of dew.

The little stars were the herring fish
That lived in that beautiful sea—
"Now cast your nets wherever you
wish — Never afraid are we";
So cried the stars to fisherman three:
Wynken,
Blynken,
And Nod.

All night long their nets they threw
To the stars in the twinkling foam —
Then down from the skies came the
wooden shoe, Bringing the fishermen
home ; 'T was all so pretty a sail it
seemed - As if it could not be,
And some folks thought 't was a dream
they'd dreamed Of sailing that beautiful sea— But I shall name you the
fishermen three:
Wynken,
Blynken,
And Nod.

Wynken and Blynken are two little
eyes,
And Nod is a little head,
And the wooden shoe that sailed the
skies Is a wee one's trundle-bed.
So shut your eyes while mother sings
Of wonderful sights that be,
And you shall see the beautiful things
As you rock in the misty sea,
Where the old shoe rocked the fisher-
men three:
Wynken,
Blynken,
And Nod.

Winken, Blinken, and Nod was my favorite song that my grandmother would sing to me.

CR

East of the Sun & West of the Moon

One winter night a large White Bear knocked on the glass pane
of a poor man's front door. The cottage was full of children,
which had one fair and lovely older daughter. The White Bear
presented the father with a transaction: He would be made a rich
man, if he would allow his beautiful daughter to accompany him
to his castle. The father agreed. (This bear was under a troll's
curse of really being a young handsome Prince. However, it was
only when sleeping that this could be seen.) Days at the castle
past and the beautiful girl grew to love the bear. However, she
inadvertently discovered that he had changed into a handsome
prince by nightfall. He knew he must then leave, to find a way to
break the spell of a curse to marry someone else.
The lovely girl sets out to follow him. She soon meets the East
Wind and West Wind who help her find three old trolls who had
gifts for her. Each gift would come in handy later to win the
White Bear back. Eventually she arrives to another castle where
a very curious woman is interested in the gifts the beautiful girl
had. This woman was preparing to be married to a handsome
prince. Her handsome Prince. She offers her gifts to the bride-
to-be; a golden apple, a carding comb, and a spinning wheel.
Each gift giving her time to be with her White Bear Prince.

However, the Prince has made it known he will only marry the girl who can get 3 tallow marks off on his special shirt. This is truly the last test the lovely girl will have to pass. The soon-to-be bride only messes up the shirt making it worse. However the beautiful girl knows exactly what to do to the shirt to have it like new again. The spell is broken. The White Bear is now his original self and marries the fair and lovely girl he met on that winter's night. Off they ride back to his castle forever happy.

De tolv villender
12 Wild Ducks

Once there was a queen with 12 sons, but her only wish was to have a daughter as white as snow and cheeks red as blood. A troll woman heard her wish and granted it, if on the day the girl is christened, all the sons would belong to her. So as it happened, her brothers became wild ducks and flew away. When the princess grew up she was often sad. She thought something was missing and asked her mother what had happened. Her mother, the queen, explained about her wish long ago and told her that she had 12 brothers. Snow White set off to find them. She walked a great distance until she came to a cottage. No one was home so she walked inside and cleaned, made a fire in the fireplace, and cooked dinner. Soon 12 ducks flew home arriving with a swooshing sound, and as they entered their doorway they became men once again. Even though she hid from them, they found her. They told her how she could set them free, by weaving hats, scarves, and shirts for them. So she did this, except she was not quite finished with one of the sleeves leaving one of the brothers with a duck wing. One day as she was walking outside a new King spotted her and asked for her hand. They were married, but the old queen was not letting their family alone. She tried to curse their daughters. However, the King was so powerful that he sent the queen far away forever. Snow White and the King and their daughters lived happily ever after.

In The Land of Odin

In the land of Odin there stands a mountain
One thousand miles in the air
From edge to edge this mountain measures
One thousand miles square.

A little bird comes wingin' once in every
Million years
Sharpens his beak on the mountain
And swiftly disappears

Thus when this mountain is finally worn away
This to Eternity will be
One single day.
As one single day.

* This ballad came out in the 60s and was sung by many different artists; Peter and Gordan, Barry McGuire, Pete Seeger and other Folk singers. Odin was considered the Nordic mythical Allfather of many gods.

A nei, sa Pete
Ei hena var mista.
Raven, han Sprang
Sa rumpa han rista.
Og nu ter jeg ikke komme
hjemma til mer.
Og nu ter jeg ikke komme
hejmma til mer.

Oh no, said Pete
A hen has gone missing.
The fox, he sprang
So his behind shook.
And now, I don't dare
Come home to mom.
And now, I don't dare
Come home to mom.

For some reason my grandmother and my mother would sing this song over and over to my brother Steve, and I. We never really knew the translation of it while we were so young, but loved to sing along anyway. It wasn't until recently that we heard the song on the internet and learned the translation.

CR

119

The KRAKEN

Once there was a Norse ship called Endurance that set sail out to sea. It's Captain, old Callahan, and crew were eager to catch fish. The sea was extremely and unusually calm that day. Endurance continued to sail further and further towards the deepest part of the ocean. Nets were put down into the water and they waited. Suddenly there was a wild abundance of fish everywhere. The crew did their best trying to pull up the nets, but long tentacles were all over the boat and themselves. You could hear the cracking of the mast and wood of the ship from the weight of the monstrous Kraken. Old Callahan mesmerized by the terror, cried as his crew submerged into the dark murky waters along with the remaining parts of his ship. He, too, sank even as his last view was of the homeland that he loved dearly.

In Norwegian sailor Folklore, KRAKEN is a legendary sea monster said to appear in the sea between Norway and Iceland. The kraken appeared in Norse Folktales and called it a Hafgufa. It was written about in travel journals and also by a missionary in the 1700s. These writings described a gigantic, squid-like creature able to pull down an entire boat or ship with it's powerful tentacles. Fact: The largest giant squid ever found was almost 43 feet long, including tentacles. It makes one wonder about the ones that were not discovered or found. In Seattle the Kraken Iceplex is a large beautiful series of ice skating rinks, for hockey practice or for fun.

Fun movie trivia: In Clash of the Titans, 2010, Zeus commands Poseidon to "Release the Kraken!". Also, in Pirates of the Caribbean: Dead Man's Chest, Davy Jones commands, "Release the Kraken".

Norwegian American Cousins Remember

Folk Ways

Det finnes ikke dårlig vær, bare dårlig klær

There is no bad weather, only bad clothing

Chapter 5

Scandinavian Fair in Solvang, California.

The young Norwegian boy is getting the wool ready by twisting the fibers, for spinning on the spinning wheel. Then the yarn will be ready for weaving.

CR

Linda's grandmother's rug.

oats

Kornband or Julenek
A Christmas Sheaf

Juleneks are always made out of oats and hung up high for the birds. Some think it's like a bribe to the birds for not destroying the next year's harvest. Or to some, it's just wanting the birds to live through the winter.

If Bullfinch and Tit birds arrive to eat the oats, it will mean the harvest will be great. If there are few birds to eat the oats? It will mean the opposite.

Many Juleneks are hung on lamp post poles in Ballard and especially near the Nordic Museum. In Poulsbo during weeks before Christmas they are also hung.

Julenek
The practice of giving a dinner for the birds
on Christmas Day

Far over in Norway's distant realm,
That land of ice and snow,
Where the winter nights are long and drear,
And the North Winds fiercely blow,
From many a low thatched cottage roof,
On Christmas Eve, 'tis said,
A sheaf of grain (julenek) is hung on high,
To feed the birds o' erhead.

This is the first verse of a 100 year old poem
by Mrs A.M. Tomlinson

Josie's hat made by Norwegian women in Ballard, WA

Needlepoint of Nepetro by Linda D.

Miniature fishing hut on the harbor
crafted by my great-uncle, Tonnes.

A rosemaled porcelain jar done by
Porsgrund porcelain fabrikk, with
nisser/trolls.

Rosemaling is the National Decorative Art of Norway. Rosemaling means rose painting.

This is a Rosemalingmeter etter original av Knut K. Hovden Stravanger Bliktrykleri 4/8 Made in Norway

CR

This was my Dad's Norwegian Folk Art important Rosemaling paper box. I inherited this. My dad had this before he married my mom, Alice Johnsen.

LD

Norwegian
stamp with
Rosemailing

Norwegian sled
with Rosemaling
CR

Rosemaling originated in the low-land areas of eastern
Norway around 1750. Painters would travel from country to country painting churches, homes, and often
painted on trunks.

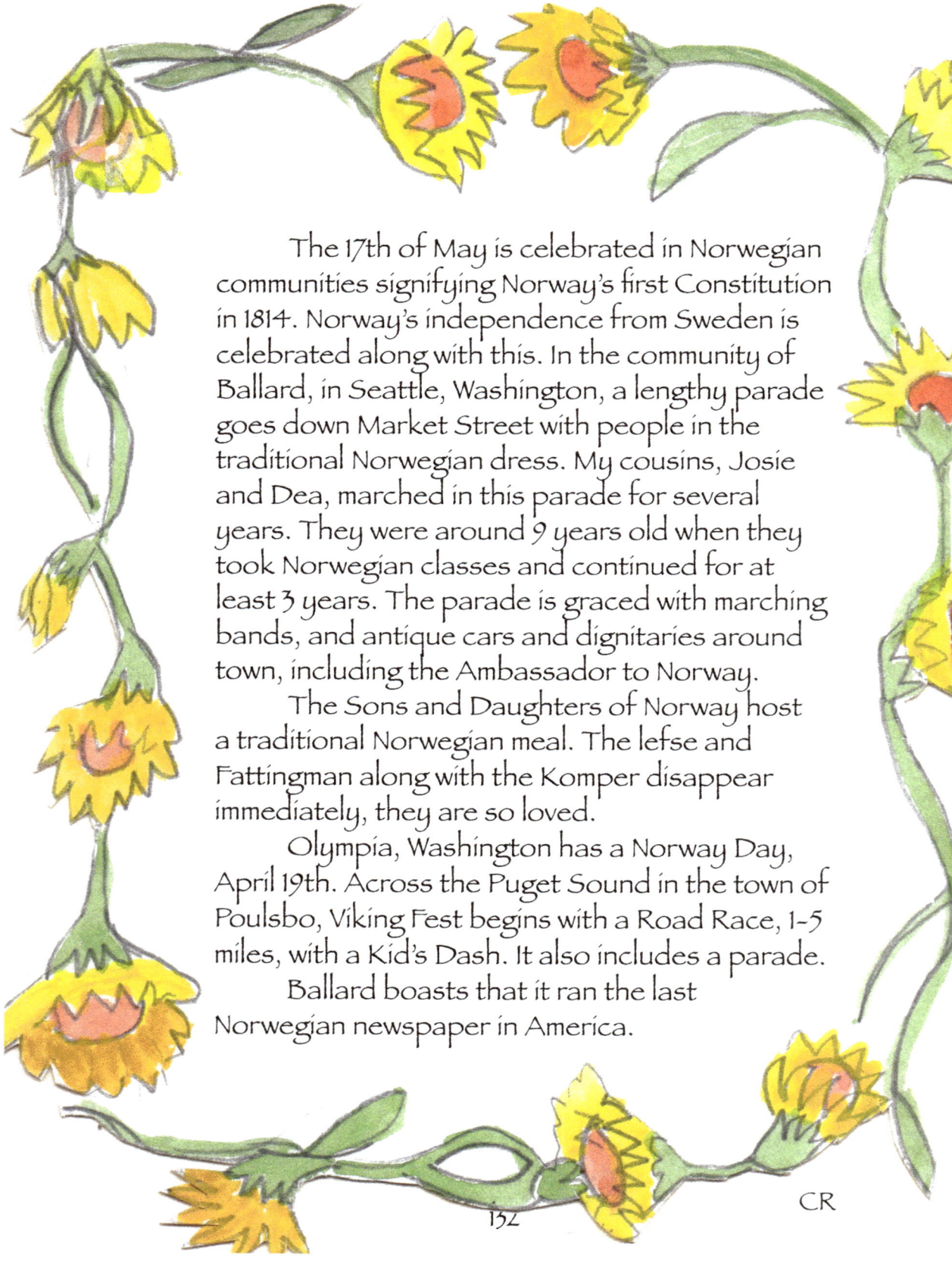

The 17th of May is celebrated in Norwegian communities signifying Norway's first Constitution in 1814. Norway's independence from Sweden is celebrated along with this. In the community of Ballard, in Seattle, Washington, a lengthy parade goes down Market Street with people in the traditional Norwegian dress. My cousins, Josie and Dea, marched in this parade for several years. They were around 9 years old when they took Norwegian classes and continued for at least 3 years. The parade is graced with marching bands, and antique cars and dignitaries around town, including the Ambassador to Norway.

The Sons and Daughters of Norway host a traditional Norwegian meal. The lefse and Fattingman along with the Komper disappear immediately, they are so loved.

Olympia, Washington has a Norway Day, April 19th. Across the Puget Sound in the town of Poulsbo, Viking Fest begins with a Road Race, 1-5 miles, with a Kid's Dash. It also includes a parade.

Ballard boasts that it ran the last Norwegian newspaper in America.

CR

Syttende Mai, photo Sons of Norway

May 17th parade Ballard
Seattle, Washington
Syttende Mai
Sons of Norway

The Traditional Norwegian Bunand

The Bunand has a white linen or cotton blouse, usually with long sleeves. A jumper-dress is worn over the blouse with a long skirt usually of wool, and black or dark shades of blue, green, brown, or maroon. This includes the vest as well, which is trimmed with narrow bands of brightly colored woven braid. This could be in cross-stitch or weaving around edges. If an apron is worn it may have vertical stripes-not too bright-often sailcloth slightly gathered. A matching purse is attached to the waist. A flowered scarf or kerchief maybe worn around shoulders. A small peaked embroidered cap tied under chin may also be worn. Tradition says that unmarried girls may put an embroidered flower or geometric design on the front too. What about shoes? Black shoes with large silver buckles go well with a silver pin at neck or even amber beads. Otherwise, none.

Linda has graciously provided a lovely picture of her mother, Alice Johnsen, in a typical traditional Bunand.

En Gate i Byen
(Ivar's Vise)
By Linda Danielsen, 1976

Jeg husker deg når jeg var liten
Over skuldrene løfta du meg
I gjennom de smal gater i byen
Ned til sommerens sjøen med deg.
Da kikka den gutt med uskyldige blikk
På den jenta som sjalv fra den kysset hun fikk.

Mange år etter når jeg traff deg igjen
På den samme smal gaten i byen.
På den kald vinters kveld, fant jeg trøst i ditt armer
Og i øyner som snakka blant blikker som varmer
Og etter du saktelig kysst meg igjen
Ble du min, for en stund, min kjaereste venn.

Husker du peiser på kald vinter kvelder?
Og turer som tok oss opp snøkappa fjeller?
Lang stille timer ved siden av sjøer?
Og varm kino kvelder ståenes i køer?
Sørlands-expessen til hytter på landet?
Og dager på kysten med utsikt mot vannet?

Men skulle du glemme de tider i sammen
De ganger med venner og gamle Norsk sanger,
Bare husk, hvis du kann, de kjaerlige ord
Den kvelden vi satt ved et Dansk Kafe' bord.
Og over musikken og sussende stemmer
Hørte jeg ord jeg aldri skal glemme.

Men byen's kafe'er spiller ikkje viser som før,
Ikkje mer av Dylan's "Knocking på Heavens Dør"
For nå er vår dager av kjaerlighet bort
Så enkelt å se hva "på gjensyn" har gjort.
Men jeg kann ikke annet en å tenke på deg

"A Street in the Town"
(Ivar's Song)
By Linda Danielsen, 1976

I remember a boy on a midsummer's night
In the town where the houses were contrasts of white
And over his shoulders he carried me down
Through the streets to the silhouetted shore of the town.
And gently he kissed my cheek in the dark,
While his eyes seemed to say,
"Farewell, you are going away".

And after the years, I saw you once more
On the same narrow street at the shore
And lingering a moment that cold winters night
I felt comfort in arms that were holding me tight.
And as your eyes laughed and you kissed me again
I became yours for a while, my sweet, sweet dear friend.

Do you remember fires on cold winters nights?
Walks through the fields up to snow covered hills?
Do you remember the many hours we sat by the fjord?
On warm summer days, or while the rain poured
Do you remember the train when we traveled up north?
Where we watched Norway's lights dance back and forth.
Then, back to the town that we both knew so well.

Well, should you forget the times that we shared
The times with good friends and singing Norse songs
Just remember one thing, those words that you spoke
While sitting at that table in the quaint Danish pub
And over the music, loud voices, and song,
You told me most dearly where my heart must belong.

But the cafes stopped playing songs like before
No more of Dylan's "Knocking on Heaven's Door"
Our days of young love, lost and mislaid.
So simple what happens when one goes away.

My Home On

PUGET SOUND

By

Rebecca Olive Erdavis.
Harda Caroline Foard.

My grandmother, Harda, and her sister, Rebecca, wrote a song together about their home in Woodway, or Edmonds, overlooking Puget Sound. They enjoyed the location so much!

I have such fond memories of visiting my great grandmother, Josine, my aunts, and Uncle Wally. My brother, Steve, and I use to explore down the hill to the beach, watch the trains go by, throw bread pieces to the seagulls, and occasionally go into the cold water.

CR

MY HOME ON PUGET SOUND
By Harda and Rebecca Erdevig

Every soul in this world has a place he holds dear
The far and wide he may roam;
Some place that always in memory brings cheer
A spot most people call home
But ambitions of life have called me away
From the spot where my heart still clings
And oft at the end of a wearisome day
I drift back on memory's wings.

In southern lands of sunshine and palms
Are scenes that delight for a time
And beauties of nature with many a charm
Are found in northernmost climbs
But there's never a spot I can call to mind
That fills me with wonderful thrills
Like those which enthrall me with many returns
Back to those western hills.

CHORUS

In my dreams of the golden sun as sinking
O'er the peaks of the purple Olympics
The skies are ablaze with rose lilac rays
Reflected in beauty on inlet and bay.
Shadows of twilight come creeping
Golden sun soon will be sleeping.
My heart at the thought gives a leap around as
I long to be back to my home on Puget Sound

Song by Harda Erdevig Foard and her sister Rebecca

139

Who really discovered America? As one travels around Seattle's suburbs the name Leif Erikson, the Norse explorer. is on public buildings, statues, and cultural centers. He is one of the famous Vikings who sailed into Newfoundland in 1,000 AD., thus the first, that we know, to discover North America. Grapes were his newly found discovery. This led Leif to name the land he discovered Vinland, later named Newfoundland. L'Anse aux Meadows, was the earliest known Viking settlement in the New World. Almost 1,000 years later in the 1960s it was discovered by a Norwegian archaeologist, Anne Ingstad and her husband Heige. When found the settlement had overgrown ruins of this ancient base camp containing three sturdy halls, various sod huts for weaving, ironworkings and ship repairs. Today there is new evidence of Viking traders further north in Greenland and Iceland following the probable Viking sailing route. The Vikings came from various parts of Scandinavia including Norway, Denmark, and Sweden and continued to explore other continents.

Leif Erikson Statue, Shilshole Bay Marina, in Seattle was a gift from the Norwegian-American Community during the Seattle's World Fair in June, 1962. Large stones form a semi-circle around the statue. Names of Scandinavians are on each stone of immigrated individuals from their homeland to Seattle, Washington.

photo by Christy Roe

Myths
Julenisse & Nisse

Nisse are small gnome-like individuals under 4 feet tall. They have an old man's face, mostly have a long white beard, red cap, wooden shoes with a wool suit and a twinkle in their eyes. They are thought to have come from Norwegian forests to live in country stables, barns and even attics. Many mountains are connected to them, too.

A long time ago nisse were thought of as a protector of the family farm. On the farm it seemed nisse helped in mysterious ways feeding the horses, cows, and live stock. They were also particularly kind to household pets and cattle. They can play tricks if they are not being treated well. If you lose your car keys or the cow's milk bucket gets tripped over you can blame it on the nisse.

Nicholas, nisse being a derivative of Nicholas, was a patron saint of children and seamen. He was known for his many kind acts toward children. Julenisse arrives Christmas Eve in Norway and is considered a supernatural being. Julenisse comes to put a gift in a sock hanging over the bed or in a shoe that would be worn the next day. A bowl of rice porridge is put out for the Julenisse Christmas Eve.

Christmas Cards and the red Nisse hat became a symbol for the Resistance when Nazi Germany occupied Norway during 1940-1945. Both were forbidden in 1942.

Norwegians have many stories about Nisse, or tricksters. They are sometimes connected with trolls. Some are big and some are tiny. I like to think that they are kind of like elves. Not all up to no good. However, their tales are often used to warn children to heed warnings.

When Uncle Wally lived in Edmonds near my grandmother and aunts, it was a very woodsy area. Fox, deer, owls, raccoons and the occasional rare sighting of a bear could be seen. So visits were full of warnings like; "don't go near the woods alone, or cross that pond, cuz sure as they said it, the nickens could get you." I believe my uncle's word for nisse was "nickens". As my older brother and I would walk around together with my uncle, he would often point in a direction of a nicken. I was always looking the wrong way and I regret that I never did see a nicken. I did hear that the tiny nisse or trolls like rice cream pudding so if you found some missing you could believe one had just been around.

CR

Trolls

The Norwegian myth version of a troll is usually different from an American troll. The troll from Norway can be quite large, be sometimes ugly, be feared, play tricks with you or even represent one of Santa's elves at Christmastime, filling your stocking with rocks or goodies. Some are thought to live in the woods or even your aunt's hay barn.

American trolls are not as versatile. They are usually pretty cute.

You can see them helping out Queen Elsa in the Disney children's movie "Frozen" and are just plain cute in the cartoon, Trolls. However, when they are trying to guard a bridge in the The 3 Billy Goats Gruff folktale, the troll is terribly hungry in wanting to eat one of the goats.

When I was growing up it was quite a fad to collect little American trolls or at least have one and make all kinds of outfits tor it. I think they even became collectors items for awhile.

Here are 2 contrasting images of trolls; an American version and a Norwegian version. Depending on your perspective they are endearing. In several European countries Troll Dolls became popular in the early 60s. Between 1963 and 1965 they were the biggest doll fad in the United States and continued to be popular in the 70s and even in the 90s.

Norwegian Trolls Linda

Linda's

Christy's

WARNING:

If traveling through troll country, it is advised to sing and laugh cheerfully, as trolls have very sensitive ears and hate the sound of merriment.

The Norwegian Troll is part of it's country's folklore and myths. It is said they are scared of lightening and church bells. The myths and stories are often taken as warnings to be careful when venturing too far into the woods, or crossing deep waters or even not showing kindness.

There was a powerful troll king, named Dovregubben, that Henrik Ibsen wrote about in his poem of Peter Gynt. A female troll was Huldra, who was said to live deep in the mountains and forests in the southeast part of Norway.

Then there is the famous troll character, Nokken, who would lure humans into the water. In "How To Train Your Dragon" (from 2010 movie) Gobber exclaims that trolls are real and that they steal your socks. (but only the left ones) Ronald Dahl, born to Norwegian parents, wrote about the challenge. the Big Friendly Giant (BFG) had to confront with the rude and troublesome trolls in his children's story. Most everyone is familiar with the "Hobbit", a J.R. Tolkien story, (English origin) where the trolls in the story were only interested in cooking and eating the hobbits.

Thomas Dambo

Corin Febus saying hello to Oscar the Bird King on Vashon Island, WA.

Charlene Roe-Swanson visiting Roskva at the Coastal Maine Botanical Garden.

Christina, Caitlin, and James visiting Jakob Two Trees in Issaquah, WA.

Thomas Dambo has created many large and kind looking troll sculptures around the world made of recycled wood. In this case, the trolls are meant to foster a connection with the environment, providing a sense of protection of nature.

Left: Corin and Christina saying hello to Frankie Feetsplinter at the Nordic Museum, Ballard, WA. Right: Kettle Point, Rhode Island, Mrs. Skipper, photo by Shannon Roe-Spence.

Bethany, Gwyneth, and Corin Febus saying hello to Pia the Peace Keeper on Bainbridge Island, WA. Vashon Island, WA.

Specialty: Blueberry Donuts
Amazing Treats
Sluys Poulsbo Bakery

Dan says, "It's like eating a handful of fresh ripe blueberries instead of bringing them home to grandma like she asked."

"Velkommen til Poulsbo"
Poulsbo, Washington
Sister City of Oslo, Norway
Ferry across the Puget Sound

CULTURAL NORDIC INFLUENCES

ART:
Edward Munch: "The Scream"
Gurhard Munthe: 19th Century Art, Pioneer of Modernism

HISTORICAL NOVELS, LOCAL LEGENDS, & STORY TELLING:
Lars Mytting

MUSIC:
Edward Gregg: Composer and Pianist, "In the Hall of the Mountain King"
ABBA: Swedish pop group formed in Stockholm

SPORTS:
Ole Gunnar Solayaer: Soccer player
Marit Bjoergen: 15 X Winter Olympic Gold Medalist skier

HUMANITARIAN:
Fridtjof Hansen: Nobel Peace Prize

PLAYWRIGHT:
Hemrik Ibsen: Peer Gynt, A Doll's House, etc.

EXPLORERS:
Leif Erikson: First European to set foot on continental North America
Thor Heyerdahl: Kon-Tiki Expedition
Roald Amundsen: First to reach South Pole

WORLD CHESS CHAMPION:
Magnus Carlsen: #1 Grandmaster for many years

CHILDREN'S BOOK AUTHOR:
Roald Dahl: Born to Norwegian Immigrant parents.
        BFG, Matilda, Charlie and the Chocolate Factory
Asbjornsen & Moe: Norwegian Folk Tales

ACTORS:
Renee Zellweger, Linda Evans, Paris Hilton, Chrissy Telgren, Kristen Wiig,
Marilyn Monroe, and Karen Black (Linda Danielsen is related to her)
Stellan skarsgard, Mads Mikkelsen, Thyra Dane, Kristoter Hivju

EDUCATIONAL NORDIC INFLUENCES

In New York City, 58 Park Ave., there is the Scandinavia House. It is called the leading center for Nordic Culture in the United States. It offers a wide variety of programs and activities. Some of these include language classes, Contemporary Nordic Art, Jazz, films, authors and more.

The National Nordic Museum on Market Street in Ballard, Seattle, Washington is a beautiful aesthetically pleasing building. It is a Scandinavian museum and cultural center with education, classes, and documentaries. Exhibits include the history as well as current culture of Nordic peoples. The gift shop has handmade items of: weaving, wood, ceramic, and glass. There are many books exemplifying their creativity. Right out front of the museum is a gigantic 20 foot troll by the artist Thomas Dambo.

The University of Washington has the country's largest Scandinavian Studies Department. There is a student exchange program at the high school level and college level with Bergen, Norway. Bergen is Seattle's Sister City. To depict this, a mural exists in Ballard's Borgen Place Park showing their friendship.

Forest School Philosophy Movement is both in Scandinavia and America. It is a play based child led exploration which is risk taking and building a strong connection with nature.

Here are some common Norwegian words and phrases.

Hello	God dag
Hi/goodbye	hei/Ha det
Do you speak English?	Snakker du engelsk
Yes/No	Ja/Nei
Please (be so kind)	vær så snill
Thank you	Takk
You're welcome	Vær så god
Can I help you?	Kan jeg hjelpe deg?
Excuse me	Unnskyld meg
(Very) good	(Veldig) bra
Farewell	Farvel
How much?	Hvor mye?
where is ... ?	Hvor er .... ?
men	menn/herrer
women/ladies	kvinner/damer
water/coffee	vann/kaffe
beer/wine	øl/vin
Cheers!	Skål!
The bill, please	Regningen, takk
Up with your chin	Opp med haken
I love you	jeg elsker deg

one two three four five six seven eight nine ten
en to tre fire fern seks sju åtte ni ti

NORDIC WISDOM

Make the most of all sunlight.

NEVER say no to the outdoors. You will be rewarded.

No such thing as bad weather, only bad clothes.

Roam free and forage freely.

Eat more fish.

Fishing yields impressive results.

Be prepared for a moose. Or the unexpected.

There is always koselig later. (similar to hygge)

Why worry when you can pray.

It's ok to take a day off with family during school hours.

Let the kids nap outside.

The seaside and beach is a wonderful playground.

Laughter is good medicine and does the heart good.

NORDIC SCENES IN MOVIES

STAR WARS - EMPIRE STRIKES BACK:
Epic battle scenes

JAMES BOND - NO TIME TO DIE:
James Bond's car chase scene

HARRY POTTER & THE HALF BLOOD PRINCE:
Winter scene where students ride the Hogwarts Express is the Rauma
Railway near Bjorli

DUNE:
Some scenes were from the Stadlandet Peninsula, Norway

THOR:
Scenes from Lofoten Islands, Norway

KON-TIKI:
Filming originates in Norway

BABBET'S FEAST:
Story set in a Norwegian village called Berlevag
(Although filmed in Denmark)

MISSION IMPOSSIBLE: FALLOUT, DEAD RECKONING
& THE FINAL RECKONING.
Multiple scenes in all of these movies were filmed in Norway.

FROZEN:
Animated him takes place in the city of Arendelle, inspired by the
city of Bergen, Norway .

The King's Choice:
Filmed in Oslo and northern Norway.

NORWEGIAN-AMERICAN HUMOR

I remember my parents would laugh together over "Ole and Sven' Jokes; The Norwegian vs. The Swede.

Here's one:
There's a lake up north that covers both the Swedish and the Norwegian border. Every winter there would be ice-fishers from both countries trying their luck. But every year the Norwegians would have a great catch, while the Swedes caught nothing. The Swedes grew a bit tired of this and decided to send a spy over to see if there was some trick the Norwegians used that they didn't know about. The spy snooped around for a bit and then came back to his side of the lake. They all gathered around him with great anticipation. He then whispered, "They drill holes in the ice."

Did you hear about the Norwegian who wore 2 jackets when he painted the house? The instructions on the can say, "Put on 2 coats."

I think this can parallel Canadian vs. United States rivalry.
What does a Canadian goose say?
"Honk, eh" or ..... "Honk, for sure"

Here's some more rivalry: Hygge vs. Kos or Koselig.
Although hygge is a Danish word, it has it's roots in Norwegian. Hygge is derived from the old Norse word "hugr", which means of the soul, mind, and consciousness.
Hygge and Koselig describe feelings of coziness, warmth and comfort in a pleasant environment.
So to create this atmosphere gather candles, music, warm drinks, simple food, blankets, pillows and fluffy stuff to enjoy company of friends and/or family.

Folksy Wisdom from Maine in the 19th Century

In all Scandinavia it is common wisdom that you can tell a lot about a person from his woodpile. Stacking the wood is an aesthetic and a practical challenge. It is said that even in the heavily forested state of Maine, Folksy Wisdom in the late nineteenth century was heeded from this list considering a potential husband by young American women.

Upright and solid pile: Upright and solid man

Low pile: Cautious man, could be shy or weak

Tall pile: Big ambitions, but watch out for sagging and collapse

Unusual shapes: Freethinking, open spirit, again, the construction may be weak

Flamboyant pile, widely visible: extroverted, but possibly a bluffer

A lot of wood: A man of foresight, loyal

Not much wood: A life lived from hand to mouth

Logs from big trees: Has a big appetite for life, but can be rash and extravagant

Pedantic pile: Perfectionist, may be introverted

Collapsed pile: Weak will, paor judge of priorities

Unfinished pile with logs l_ying on the ground: Unstable, lazy, prone to drunkenness.

Everything in a pile on the ground: Ignorance, decadence, laziness, drunkeness, possibly all of these.

old and new wood piled together: .E>esu spicious: might br stolen wood added to his own

Large and small logs piled together: Frugal. Kindling sneaked in among the logs suggests a considerate man

Rough, gnarled logs, hard to chop: Persistent and strong willed, or else bowed down by his burdens

No woodpile: No husband

Folksy Wisdom from "NORWEGIAN WOOD" BY LARS MYTTING

Just to name a few Norwegian and Scandinavian places that you will enjoy

Jule Hus
1580 Mission Dr.
Solvang, CA. 93463
Handcrafted traditional
Scandinavian Items

Lulu Hyggelig,
Thomas Dambo troll
California Nature Art Museum
1511 Mission Dr.
Solvang, CA. 93463

Scandinavian Festival
60 W. Olsen Rd.
Thousand Oaks, CA. 91360

Byen Bakery
15 Nickerson Ave.
Seattle, Wa. 98109

Sluys' Bakery
18924 Front St. NE
Poulsbo, WA. 98370

Viking Fest of Little Norway
Waterfront Park, May 17th
19735 10th Ave.
Poulsbo, WA. 98370

Larsen's Bakery
Handcrafted Traditional
Scandinavian Bakery
8000 24th Ave. NW
Seattle, WA. 98117

National Nordic Museum
2655 NW Market St.
Seattle, WA. 98107
History, Arts and Crafts,
Cafe, and troll by Thomas Dambo
Frankie Feet Splinters

Freya Bakery and Cafe
Below Pike's Market
1426 Western Ave.
Seattle, WA. 98101

Nutty Norsky Baking Co.
Skagit's Own Fish Market
18042 WA-20
Burlington, WA. 98233

Olsen's Scandinavian Foods
2248 NW Market Street
Seattle, WA 98107
Food, clothing, trolls, gifts
Founded by Norwegians

House of Norway
Balboa Park
661 Pan American W,Rd.
San Diego, CA 92101
History, culture and traditions
Leif Erikson Day Oct. 9th

Norway Day in Olympia
Thurston County Fairgrounds
Olympia, WA.
3rd Weekend in April

Scandinavia House
The Nordic Center in America
58 Park Ave.
New York, NY 10016

Mostly Nordic
17205 Vashon Hwy SW
Vashon Island, WA 98070

Smør Bakery
437 E. 12th Street
New York, NY 10009

A Little Info on Christy Roe

My mother and grandmother's Norwegian language, recipes, and stories gave me a curiosity and love for Nordic culture. I have always wanted to learn more about this beautiful heritage of peoples whom I'm related to. My adult daughters know a little of this influence just by living in Seattle with it's surrounding Scandinavian communities.

I am a teacher, artist, mother and grandmother with a love of the ocean, books, and family.

Co-leading workshops in Santa Fe, New Mexico and Spain has given me an appreciation for more cultures.

Communicating with Linda on the information we have gathered to share in this book has been enjoyable. Hopefully, it will stir up fond memories for each person reading this as well.

I hope to visit my relatives in Lillisand to hear more history and learn new recipes someday.

Christy Roe-Merwin

Christy Roe with her brothers
John, Steve. Dan, and Tim.

A Little Info on Linda Danielsen

I consider myself more Norwegian than American. I grew up following Norwegian traditions in the highty populated Norwegian Bay Ridge district of Brooklyn and in Huntington, Long Island. As a result, I speak fluent Norwegian. It was the first language I learned, and continued to speak Norwegian, especially together with my grandmother and grandfather.

I am a scientist and a professor. My science degree enabled me to have an exciting career. I worked at one of the first biotech companies, which participated in groundbraking research in cloning and gene sequencing, and I also worked at the first private DNA forensics company, where we used DNA as a forensic tool.

This project was extremely enjoyable. I was able to share much of my ancestry research with Christy, as well as my knowledge of Lillesand, Norway. My ancestry goes all the way back to the 800s and it also shows that I am related to famous Viking kings. Christy and I were able to share Norwegian recipes that our mothers and grandmothers brought over to the U.S. from Norway. I agree with Christy that Christmas is especially a magical time since we both celebrate a traditional Norwegian Christmas. It was fun to share the different memories we both had. I have never lost touch with my relatives who live in Norway. My first cousins and their offspring are so welcoming whenever I or my son visit.

Linda Danielsen with her mother Alice
and brothers Lloyd, John, Glenn, and Tom.

PERMISSIONS

THOMAS DAMBO:
Troll Sculptures:
www.thomasdambo.com
& www.trollman.com

OG SJÖFARTSMUSEET
MUSEUM:
"Mitilde" book cover from Anne
Sophie, Lillesand, Norway

SYLTENDE MAY:
May 17th parade photo, Sons of
Norway, Seattle, WA

STEVE ROE:
Letter and photos

DAN ROE:
Quote Sluys Bakery, Blueberry
Donut

BYEN BAKERY:
Photo of Julekake. Nickerson Ave,
Lower Queen Anne, Seattle, WA

SLUYS BAKERY, POULSBO:
Illustration of logo

DEBBIE ERDEVIG:
Photo and recipe

JOSIE LEHDE:
Letter, photo, and recipes

BETHANY, CORIN, AND
GWYNETH FEBUS:
Photo with Troll and Dutch Baby

CHRISTINA MERWIN:
Photos

CHARLENE SWANSON and
daughter Shannon:
East Coast Troll photos

LINDA FOARD:
Photos

MARIT DANIELSEN:
Folkways and photos

ARNE DANIEL TANDBERG :
Photo of Family Reunion

MARTY DEGRAZIA :
Christmas Poem By Marty's
Mother.

LARS MYTTING :
"Folksy Wisdom"

Linda Danielsen's
grandparents on her
mother's side:

Christy Roe's great
grandparents on her
mother's side:

Acknowledgments

Many thanks to all of those who
contributed photos, trips, history
and favorite recipes.

Josie, Debbie, Dan, Steve, Marit,
Linda F., Clara, Charlene, Shannon, Edna,
Corin, Gwyneth, Bethany
our mothers Carol and Alice,
and our grandmothers Harda and Mathilde

A special hug and thanks to my
daughter Christina for all her patience and
hard work getting this published.

Tro, håp og kjærlighet

Faith, hope and love

Index

A

Aebleskiver 52, 53
Akake 57
Ancestry 1
A nei, sa Pete 119
Asbjornsen & Moe 99, 150

B

Berliner Kranser 42
Blueberry Donuts 148
Bunand 134, 135

C

CRAB DIP 92

D

Daniel Danielsen XIV, XV
De tolv villender 115
Dutch Baby 35, 54, 55, 56, 57

E

East of the Sun & West of the Moon 112
Erdevig 5

F

Fattigmann 28, 58
FISH CAKES 76
Folktales 97
Folk Ways 123
FRUIT SOUP 65

G

gnome 142

H

Hans Danielsen 4, 12, 18, 21
Hans Kristian Sorensen XIV
Harda Erdevig 5, 14, 98
Havrekjekks 50
Herring 89
Holiday Desserts 39
Humor 155

I

In The Land of Odin 117
Ivar's Song 137

J

JULEKAKA 63
Julenek 37, 126, 127
Julenisse 37, 142, 143

K

King Crab 90
Komper 81, 132
KRAKEN 120
Kransekake 41
Krumkaker XV, 28, 42, 49

L

Lapskaus 27, 77
LARS MYTTING 156
Lefse 28, 37, 82, 83, 84, 85, 132
Leif Erikson 140
Lillisand 10, 25
Linda Danielsen XIV, XV, 136

lobster 9, 11, 70, 71
Lutefisk 37, 42, 85

M

Marty DeGrazia 32
MOVIES 154
MY HOME ON PUGET SOUND 139

N

Nettle Star Bread 87
Nettle Tea 86
Nisse 46, 129, 142, 143
NOBEL PEACE PRIZE 2
NORDIC INFLUENCES 150, 151
NORDIC WISDOM 153

O

Ole Hansen Erdevig 21
OSLO 2

P

Pear Mousse 94
Pepperkaker 61
Princess On A Glass Hill 107

R

Rabarbrasuppe 66
Raspeball 79
RED FRUIT SAUCE 47
RIS KREM 47
Rosemaling 130, 131
Rosettes 45
Rullepolse 28, 74

S

Sage Breaded Dressing 75
SANDKAKER 51
Serina Kaker 60
Sluys Poulsbo Bakery 148
Snelldalen 7, 10, 21, 24
SOT SUPPE 64
Steve Roe, Letter 22
SVISKER GROT 67
Syttende Mai 133

T

Table Prayer 38, 68
TANTE CLARA 44
The Boy who Went to The North Wind 104
The Three Billy Goats Gruff 102
The White Bear King Valemon 109
Thomas Dambo 146, 147
TRIPP TRAPP TRESSKO 103
Trolls 37, 99, 109, 112, 144, 145
Turkey 72, 73

W

Why the Sea Has Salt 101
Winken, Blinken, and Nod 110